The Value Creation Bible for The Mid-Market

Kibel, Harvey R.

The Value Creation Bible For The Mid-Market

ISBN 0-9628399-2-2

To Isabel, Ellen, Paul, Karen,
George, Natalie and Emily

Contents

Preface

This book is intended as a comprehensive guide to all of those mid-market companies that have been struggling to create value for their business. Who are these mid-market companies? I have defined them as public and private companies with annual revenues between $10 million and $1.5 billion. They are the companies often ignored by the large consulting firms who focus their primary efforts on the Fortune 1000. They are the public companies ignored by Wall Street. We call these public companies *orphans*. Yet some mid-market companies do get recognized and command extremely high valuations, while most flounder. This is a *how to* book, no matter what stage of development your business finds itself.

The First Chapter explains the **Value Creation** process by tracking the reader through an Exhibit capturing the important milestones in the process.

Chapter Two emphasizes the importance of personal goals and objectives and shows you a lifelong process that always works. This is a key chapter because your company goals are nothing but a subset of your personal goals.

Chapter Three takes up a good part of the book and is the secret of longtime **Corporate Health**. It is the **Corporate Clock** that we have effectively used with over 1,000 clients. It tells you where you are on the **Corporate Clock** and explains the different phases from: **Healthy** to **Crossroads** to **Conflict** to **Crisis**. It shows you how to find out the time at your business and gives you a process for migrating back to the **Healthy** quadrant. A company must first be **healthy** if it is going to create real long-term value.

Chapter Four explores the impact of the Technology Revolution of **Value Creation**. Executives today must understand the dramatic impact of technology if they are to survive in the long run.

Chapter Five briefly describes the Preliminary Assessment. The purpose of this assessment is to identify the company's potential for breakthrough changes in valuation through either improvement of the *core* business or the creation of major paradigm shifts.

Chapter Six describes the process for developing the **Value Creation Plan**. It looks at potential areas such as globalization, joint ventures, strategic alliances, key acquisitions, utilization of technology, and emphasizes the importance of top management support and having the right team.

Chapter Seven discusses the problems of implementation. It is one thing to design a Plan, another to implement, when that implementation often involves a change in the corporate culture. **Value Creation** implementation is not a *white glove* process, it is *hands on* and not for the faint hearted.

Finally, Chapter Eight shows the connection between **Value Creation** and the planning of an Exit Strategy. The two are inseparable because **Value Creation** should always precede exiting since the main idea is to maximize the value of the entity one is planning to exit.

I call this book a bible because it covers all the important areas of the **Value Creation** process and I hope has taken out some of the magic. You will go back to certain chapters for inspiration and for practical *how to* information as you go through this all important process.

The content of this book is useful for owners and key executives of mid-market companies. It is also useful for professionals who advise these firms. Students can get in on the ground floor of what I believe will be a key skill needed by all future executives. Investors can use the ideas here to identify *orphan* public companies that are currently undervalued.

I hope this book opens your eyes to the wonderful opportunity that is presently sitting right under your nose.

I want to thank Paulette Rua, Claire Grossman and my long time editor Sheila Hutman for their ideas and input, and my wife Isabel for living with someone who likes to write.

Harvey R. Kibel

What Is The Value Creation Process?

Chapter 1

My fundamental thesis is that **Value Creation** occupies the center of a much bigger issue: what to do with your life and your business. Simply put, no matter what you intend to do, maximizing the value of your business is a critical early step in the process. If you knew today that you could double, triple, or increase your business six-fold in the near future, you would initiate action to bring that about before considering other strategies. This ability to increase value significantly, with the help of this book, is clearly within your grasp. Creating value today is far more complex because the old rules of relying on growth and profits no longer suffice. Even the recent run up of the market followed by a sell off, when analyzed carefully, reveals that solid businesses with good growth and earnings, but without the connection to new technology, did not increase in value as a group over this past year. Therefore, it is necessary for us to take a careful look at the entire process, which is illustrated in Exhibit A.

A business is a means to an end. It is part of the process that will enable you to achieve your personal goals. These goals involve more than maximizing the value of your

1

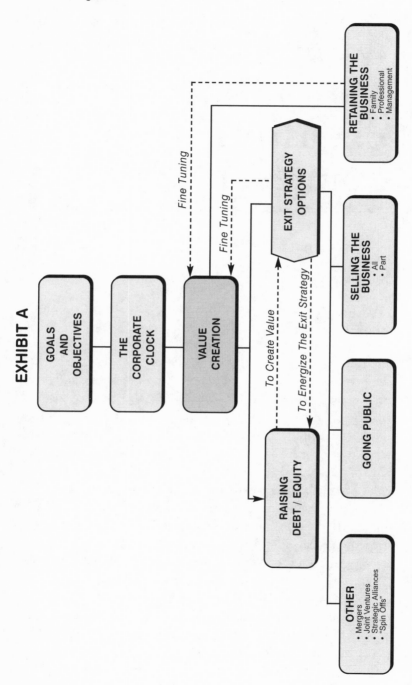

EXHIBIT A

business (although this is an important part). They include your career, investments, personal growth, social activities, hobbies, health maintenance, family time, and other general life style considerations. Your goals must be clearly understood. Your life is like a piece of clay, and you are the artist. Only you can make your life a beautiful work of art. Life doesn't happen to you — you make it happen. In this book, I will describe a process for setting these goals in a way that will give your life balance and serenity. Once you see your path clearly and know how to get there, good things will come your way. You will understand the old adage: "It is better to be prepared for an opportunity than to have an opportunity for which you are unprepared." Your goals will impact your Exit Strategy or your desire to retain the business. They will also determine your taste for risk and expansion. If, for example, you are locked into your *core* business as your only option for **Value Creation**, you will come up with a different answer than if you were open to paradigm shifts.

In carrying out the goal setting and tactic setting process, I strongly suggest that you go off by yourself. I also strongly suggest that you show these goals to no one. This advice is the product of long experience watching executives set goals that will please their fellow executives, families and community. Unfortunately, the goals do not reflect the individual's deep-seated personal desire to accomplish things that are private or that others may consider selfish. You leave these goals out of your life at the expense of your soul.

Now, let us assume that the goals and objectives along with the means of achieving them have been completed to your personal satisfaction. Now it is time to take stock of your business. Where are you now? Most executives have an overly optimistic view of their business. Therefore, I introduce a process for determining its state of **health**. We use the **Corporate Clock** for this purpose. The **Clock** has four basic quadrants: **Healthy, Crossroads, Conflict** and **Crisis**. There are many sub-categories within each major quadrant. For example, the **Healthy** quadrant is composed of both **healthy-healthy** companies and **healthy-lucky** companies. The **Crisis** quadrant has a **Red Zone** at 11:30 PM when it is too late to fix anything.

A series of questions extracted from the 49-page analysis tool used by our consultants enables you to determine in what quadrant your business is functioning. This is important because if your business is not in a **healthy-healthy** state, steps must first be taken to get the business there as soon as practical. There is no point in trying to maximize the value of an unhealthy business. It is important to attend to this matter of moving to good **health** promptly because time accelerates as a business moves around the **Clock**. For example, a business in a **Crisis** appears to be moving 30 times faster than a **healthy-healthy** company. Daily reports replace monthly reports and putting out fires, rather than planning for the future, becomes the main occupation. Once the goals are determined and the *core* business brought to **health**, it is time to look at the issue of **Value Creation**.

The process of **Value Creation** will be covered in Chapters Five, Six and Seven. It involves a general assessment of the company to determine how to (1) maximize the *core* business and (2) generate new opportunities by creating new products or services for existing customers or creating new customers for existing products. The second and less comfortable part of the process is to consider major shifts in the way a company conducts its business. This could involve e-commerce, connecting with the Internet and/or utilizing some other new technology. The preliminary assessment would involve looking for a major breakthrough for increasing value.

Once these breakthroughs are identified, the next task is to design a **Value Creation Plan**. These ideas must then be put to the test. The company must have the financial and human resources to carry out the program. Management must also have the courage to implement the change. Change is never easy, particularly if that change takes management out of its *core* competency. The Plan could involve selling off portions of the business, making selective acquisitions, creating the proper infrastructure to support a massive expansion, or examining globalization opportunities, strategic alliances, and joint ventures. It may be necessary to raise capital, install a new **Value Creation** incentive system, develop training programs and change the organization structure. Key management must be involved in the creation of the **Value Creation Plan** from the beginning because they must buy into the entire program. Objections must be considered and all risk versus reward issues fully analyzed to insure that the program is not approved from the top down, only to be sabotaged from the bottom up. The Plan must be detailed with established milestones. The *core* business must not be sacrificed while the changes are being implemented. There is an art to running this *project* structure while the *process* structure of the *core* business is being managed. The *oversight* structure, therefore, becomes very important. Finally comes the hard task of implementation: new funding must be found; a new incentive system installed; the company reorganized; the information highway built into the business; the fulfillment function put in place; and new products and/or services brought on board. All of this must occur while the *core* business is being managed.

As the Plan begins to be implemented and pieces of it are working, it is necessary to properly inform the outside world what has been done. Poor communication can adversely affect value even if the Plan is working from an operational point of view.

Returning to Exhibit A, we see the interaction between **Value Creation** and Exit Strategy, and **Value Creation** and the raising of debt and/or equity. Sometimes it is necessary to bring in new capital to complete the **Value Creation Plan**. This, in turn, may bring in new equity investors who must be evaluated in light of one's personal desires for control. The Exit Strategy itself may be subject to fine-tuning based on value. If, for example, the value of the business can be increased ten-fold by going public, that may become an option even though initially it was rejected. The raising of debt may solve the problem, but at the expense of leveraging the business. This could affect your comfort zone in the other direction. Control versus safety is an issue that cannot be resolved by analysis alone. One must consider other personal and sometimes family issues.

As the above problems are resolved, it becomes easier to examine exit strategies. Many owners or executives say to me, "I am not planning to exit, so why bother." My answer is simple. "Always have your company prepared to be sold." There are important reasons for this. First of all, circumstances may force you (health, conflicts, etc.). Second, the markets may be right. If you are not prepared, you will miss the window of opportunity. Finally, having your business always ready for sale will insure that it is being run in the best possible manner. It will force you to have good management and a strong infrastructure, as well as a clear working strategy and direction. It will also encourage you to pay attention to such outside market forces as capital markets, competition and the economy.

Before discussing the more traditional exit strategies, the option of retaining the business must be examined. Buying and holding the business is a valid strategy. It is a way of insuring control and works best for companies that generate significant cash flow. This is not a good solution for poorly advised executives who are stuck with unmarketable companies because of the way the business has been organized. An owner may want to leave the business to a member of the family or to employees, or he may decide to hire professional management and thereby retain control without the pressure of day-to-day operations. In the latter case, it is important to turn over the management to a *rainmaker,* not to someone who has never been first in command. (For a complete definition of a *rainmaker,* see Chapter Two.)

If the business is being turned over to a family member, make certain the individual is competent to lead no matter how close you are to them. Confirm that they want the job and share a common vision with you. If employees are to take over the business, be sure the deal is properly structured. Give consideration to an employee ESOP (Employee Stock Ownership Plan). Make certain the business going forward is not put at risk.

Sometimes value can be created through size and control of the marketplace. A first, second or third ranking company is worth a lot more than a business that has a small share of the market. Size can be achieved through acquisition, but this can be expensive and there may be control issues. If the company is able to get a very high multiple *after* going public, it may be better to delay expansion until then and make acquisitions with possibly over-valued stock. A business may want to consider spinning off some of its divisions. For example, a high technology division of a traditional "bricks and mortar" company might be assigned a different value as a *stand-alone* business. In other words, the total value of the "bricks and mortar" company plus the value of the new high technology company may be worth more than the value of the entity as a *hybrid* business. I know this defies logic, but that is the nature of the **Value Creation** business.

If the business is short of capital and can't readily utilize its stock as currency, then strategic alliances should be a consideration. These alliances, formed with the right synergy, can allow for rapid growth at a lower cost. Nothing is free, and these alliances often suffer from severe issues of control and communication. It is important that they be properly structured. They must be perceived as fair, or they will fall apart in the long run.

There are times when it is better to create a new venture, fund it properly, and bring in mutually agreed upon management so that it can be run with minimum interference from the participating companies. Again, proper structuring is very important.

There are a lot of locker room conversations about going public. Everybody has heard about someone who made many millions of dollars by going public. When the market is right and you are in the right business at the right time, going public can be wonderful. Here are some things, however, that you need to know.

- First, going public can be expensive. The accounting and legal fees alone can run well over $500,000 to $1 million *and* there is no guarantee the deal will come off at the right price. Moreover, if the market begins a rapid decline, there is no guarantee that the deal will happen at all.

- Second, you need to make sure there is a support system in place for your stock. You need institutions and retail houses to promote the stock after it has gone public, or you may find the value declining even if you are performing well operationally. I know of an excellent management team that has met every target and grown the business over the past five years by over 700%, yet the stock has dropped by 60%! This, too, defies logic. That is why the **Value Creation** business is a complex science with a little bit of art mixed in for good measure.

- Finally, you need to recognize that floodlights are now on the business. Irate shareholders may question your compensation and your competence. The SEC (Securities and Exchange Commission) requires many timely reports. You have to be available to answer questions not only from shareholders, but also from the very sophisticated people on Wall Street. Heaven help you if you fail to meet a projection. You'd better have a good explanation.

Nevertheless, going public can sometimes yield the highest

valuation for the business and give you useful currency to attract excellent talent and to make deals.

Many owners of companies have too much of their net worth tied up in their business. They may not want to get out, nor want to go public, but still want to be more liquid. The best answer here is to sell part of the company to the right kind of buyer. That, of course, is the major issue. Will the buyer be in management? If so, you have acquired a partner as well as an investor. Are you willing to sell a controlling interest? If so, you have given up the right to really manage the destiny of your business. If you are selling a minority interest, the buyer will be concerned about protection in case you don't perform. Nothing is simple.

This, then, is the process. Now I hope you can understand why **Value Creation** is so important. Yet most executives neglect this because they believe they are best qualified to maximize value. As a result, they will leave many millions of dollars on the table that could have gone into their pockets.

Chapter 2

Personal Goals and Objectives

When I wrote my first book, *How to Turn Around a Financially Troubled Company,* I became aware that failing companies followed certain common patterns. It further became apparent that owners and key executives also exhibited common traits. If there is a blueprint for failing, I concluded, maybe there is a pattern for succeeding in life. *Success* is an elusive word. It is not easy to define, but it is easy to know when you are in the presence of a successful person. What is it that we see in such people?

- High self-esteem.

- A sense of direction.

- An ability to work with and through others to get what they want.

- Sufficient financial success to lead the kind of life they desire.

- Vibrant health and high energy.

- A sense of excitement and awareness of the world around them and an understanding of how it all connects to their lives.

- A willingness to take risks.

In my many years with the Young Presidents' Organization, my years as a Partner with Peat, Marwick, Mitchell & Company, and my dealings with successful executives, I became aware that the above traits were common to most of these special people. Many of them learned these skills. Contrary to popular belief, they were not born with them.

I call such people *rainmakers*. They see life as a process, take full responsibility for it, and place great value on each minute of their existence. I know this book can help you to be the *rainmaker* of your own life process.

IDENTITY

Who are you? Why have you been put on this earth? What has been important in your past? Is there a pattern? What are your strengths? What are your weaknesses? Can you be truly honest with yourself? The time for playing games with the world must now come to an end. Believe me, it is hard to break the habit of playing games. Games protect you from others and, most importantly, prevent you from dealing with yourself as a truly complex human being with both good and bad traits. We cannot begin to talk about goal setting without an identity review, which must in the final analysis involve the accepting and the embracing of ourselves completely. This requires loving yourself — your faults and your weaknesses. Your self-love must be unconditional!

How do we begin this process? It is simple. Decide today

that sometime in the next two weeks you will take off one complete day *by yourself.* You will travel away from home to an area where you will be undisturbed for 24 hours! Your spouse, lover, and/or friends will be jealous or, possibly, think you are crazy. Since one of our objectives is to free ourselves from seeking the approval of others, this first step is excellent practice for you. Remember, if you were ill, you would take time off to recuperate. Taking time off to accomplish this task will kick off a program that will lead to a longer, healthier life filled with quality, vitality and enjoyment. Now I ask you again, "Can you make the one-day investment?"

You are now on your way to your 24-hour Shangri-La with some homework assignments I have given you. Clear your mind of all current problems (spouse, children, lover, business, friends, health, etc.). In time, you will look at each of them in detail — both rationally and emotionally. One basic rule you must follow is that the information you will prepare is to be shared with *no one.* I repeat — *no one.* You must be completely honest with yourself, and if you think for a moment that someone else will ultimately review these notes, it will affect your honesty. You must be truthful — there is no point in fooling yourself. I just can't emphasize this point enough. The rest of the world will go on fulfilling its own needs, but you will not be there fulfilling yours unless you are brutally honest. (Have I lectured enough?)

Now take out a sheet of paper and list in detail what you believe to be your major weaknesses. (You may prefer to use a laptop or palm-size computer but, for purposes of this exercise, handwriting may be more effective.) Remember, be honest and leave nothing out. It doesn't matter how you think the world sees you. All that matters is what you think. Here are some areas and points to consider:

• Role as father, mother, husband, wife, lover;

• Condition of health — mental and physical;

- Quality of your friendships;

- Lack of satisfaction with economic status;

- Lack of motivation;

- Inability to relax;

- Dependence on others for approval;

- Satisfaction with status of career;

- Happiness with your work;

- Fear of risk and the future;

- Unfamiliarity with new technology;

- Lack of outside interests;

- Weakness in financial planning;

- Fear of confrontation;

- Lack of fun in your life; and

- Inability to organize your time.

The above list is far from exhaustive. In fact, it would defeat our purpose merely to give you a checklist. Ask yourself the questions that hurt. What do you wish you could do over? Would you have *you* for a friend? Look in the mirror. What do you see that displeases you? This is you — a human being — who must own up to all your deficiencies. Some areas may make you cry. *Go ahead* — it's good for you. This task probably will not be pleasant, but for some of you it may be the first time in your life you have honestly *soul searched.* When the list is complete, look at the items carefully. Have you left anything out? Do the deficiencies *fit?*

Next, take the list and prioritize these deficiencies. The top of the list will include those areas that disturb you the most, that make you unhappy, that interfere with your life. The bottom of the list contains those deficiencies you can tolerate. Take the completed list and put it aside. Clear your head, take a 30-minute walk, and just enjoy the outdoors. Let your mind and feelings roam free. Can you feel that something has happened to you already? Come back and read the list again. This is you at your worst. Not really a bad person at all. In fact, while you (like the rest of us) have deficiencies, you are human (like everyone else) with rights to a place on this planet!

Now take out another sheet of paper and list in detail what you believe to be your major strengths. Be honest. Remember, no one but you will ever see these sheets. Again, list your strong points as *you* see them — not as you believe others see them. Consider your health, the quality of your friendships, economic and career satisfactions, outer or inner directedness, technical skills, willingness to risk, etc.

Next, take the list and prioritize these strengths. The top of the list will include those in which you take great pride, the characteristics you know you can always fall back on when life is not going very well. Clear your head and again take a 30-minute walk. Keep yourself as relaxed, and your mind as free, as possible. Return to your retreat and reread the list of strengths. This represents you at your best — as *you see you.* Now tape the strengths and weaknesses sheets together, placing the strengths sheet on your left and the deficiencies sheet on your right. You are looking at your personal balance sheet as of today. Read it carefully. Have you left anything out? Does it feel right? Does it describe you as you are now? Do you understand that everyone has such a personal balance sheet? Most people, however, have not taken this all-important first step. While you may desire to add new strengths and rid yourself of certain deficiencies, you must first accept yourself just as you are — unconditionally! You are human; you are not perfect. There will always be strengths and there will always be deficiencies, although the specifics may change. Life is a dynamic process that ends only with death. It is time, therefore, to stop waiting for a particular change to occur before you love yourself completely and absolutely. Unless you do this, you cannot love others except out of desperate need, rather than want. Relationships based on such a thin thread soon fall apart.

We are now ready to begin our third homework assignment: identifying the important milestones in your life. The easiest way to carry out this exercise is to take out a third sheet of paper and, on the left side, record your age from year one to the present. Go back over your life and list all the milestones. Which events made you extremely happy? Which made you very sad? What raised your self-confidence? What happened that made you feel a loss of power, etc.? Below are some examples of the kinds of milestones that may have affected you.

- Experiencing the death of a loved one

- Having a near fatal accident

- Winning a major sports event

- Applying for something and being or not being selected

- Getting or losing an important job

- Failing a course

- Falling in love

- Getting married or divorced

- Suffering from a major health problem

- Discovering a painful secret

- Receiving a major promotion or demotion

- Gaining or losing an important friend

- Having a child

- Leaving home

- Losing your children

- Facing a major financial gain or setback

The list is endless. Hopefully, the suggestions above will start your thoughts moving in the right direction. The further back in time you go, the harder it will be to remember. Stop, walk, think back — try to understand your life history and, most importantly, to recall how you responded emotionally to each milestone in your life. Let your greatest fear unmask itself. Remember, no one but you will ever see these sheets of paper. Own your own fear and your own triumphs. They all contributed to making you what you are today. Because you have already completed a *strengths and weaknesses* analysis, the milestone reflections will flow quite rapidly.

At last we come to the final assignment before goal setting. I hope you have not eaten anything yet. Food will be your reward after this next assignment, which should be somewhat enjoyable.

On a fourth sheet of paper, allow yourself to consider all the things you would like to be, all the traits you would like to have, and the careers you would like to pursue. Please do not permit red lights to inhibit your thinking. Don't filter something out because you feel you're not good enough, too old, too young, too short, too fat, too dumb, too sullen, too badly coordinated, too slow, too poor, or too disorganized. Remember that Beethoven was too deaf to write music, Napoleon too short to lead a great nation, Einstein too dumb in school to amount to anything, Lincoln too poor to consider a lofty position, Grandma Moses too old to paint . . . need I go on? It is time to begin to remove limits. This final list will be edited at a later time, *not now*. Let your mind run free like that of a child. I want to release in you the child that dares to dream about a better tomorrow. Thinking, dreaming and visualizing will become a permanent part of your life now that you have taken this first step. In completing this list, it is often helpful to think of people you admire. Which of their traits inspire you?

Congratulations on the completion of Phase I! Time for some food, but look over your homework papers while you eat. Reread them, etch them into your mind, and make them a dynamic part of you. They provide the first insights into who you are. Promise yourself that this person, just as he/she is, with all of his/her weaknesses and strengths, with all of the experiences that have shaken his/her life, with all of his/her dreams is worthy of your love. Your love of yourself should be unconditional. It resembles the love of a parent for a child — unwavering, yet wanting to be certain that the child has unlimited opportunities for growth, fulfillment and happiness. Other people may come and go in your life — but you must be there for yourself all of the time. You deserve all the goodness the world has to offer.

GOAL SETTING

When you return home, you may be quite pensive. Possibly a week has passed during which you have been reviewing, editing, adding, modifying and deleting the information developed at your retreat. Who you are is becoming clearer as you begin the process of peeling away each protective layer to reach your essential *core*. A desire to realize yourself as a person will surge within you. Purchase a package of 3" x 5" cards. You will use them for goal setting. Your basic approach to goal setting will be as follows:

1. State the goal precisely, including dates of completion, quantity data, etc. The goal must be very specific. Instead of saying, for example, "I want to be rich," say, "I will increase my net worth to $10.0 million by April 3, 2005." Or, "I will earn $1.0 million per year by June 15, 2003."

2. Sit back and visualize the goal as if you already possess it. If net worth were part or your entire goal, how would your life be different? where would you live? what would your family and social life be like? how would you spend your day? etc. Make certain your vision is very clear. The clarity of the picture enhances the probability of goal achievement.

3. Ask yourself if the picture feels good. If it does, the goal is probably a beneficial one for you. If it doesn't, either the goal must be changed or the picture in your mind modified.

4. Recognize that every goal requires effort on your part for its achievement. Nothing in this world comes free. Ask yourself if you are willing to *give* for this goal in order to *get* the benefits its achievement has to offer.

5. Write the goal down on a 3" x 5" card in clear and concise language. No hedging. There must be no way out. You cannot get across or down the river if your boat is

still docked at the shore. The first step in committing yourself to a goal is analogous to untying the rope from the dock. The completion of the journey is not guaranteed — there are risks, but you will face those risks with a plan to guide you. Sometimes, unexpected surprises will come your way.

6. Write *each* goal in similar format on a separate 3" x 5" card. I strongly suggest that you establish goals in many areas so that your life has balance. Consider such areas as:

- Career;

- Economics and investments;

- Friends and social activities;

- Hobbies and outside interests;

- Family and children;

- Personal growth and development; and

- Health.

7. Reread each of these goals carefully. Make certain that you can visualize each goal clearly. See yourself in your goals as if they had already been achieved. I would suggest a small number of goals. Now prioritize them. Each goal must rank as more or less important than the others. Horizontal goal setting, wherein all goals are approximately equal, is a method guaranteed to drive you crazy. You will spend your life running around like a chicken without a head unless you see the relative importance of each goal clearly. This is critical because,

as you go through life, there will be many times when you will have to choose between goals with little time to process the decision. Therefore, that tradeoff must be fixed indelibly in your mind long before such a choice is necessary.

8. Now rank your 3" x 5" cards in order of importance. You are ready to consider the tasks required to accomplish the goals. I believe the easiest approach is to visualize the goal clearly and precisely, look at your strengths and weaknesses, the milestones in your life, and your dreams. Think of the goal as point B and your present status as point A. You want to move from point A to point B. The tasks are merely a statement of the work required to get there. The tasks must be specific and follow a logical sequence. Remember, some projects must be done in sequence; some in parallel. Sometimes others can do a project for you, and some may already have been done. You may not need to look any *further than your nose* for answers. Sometimes a given task can assist you toward more than one goal. Be on the alert for this.

9. Record the tasks on the back of the 3" x 5" card.

Read and reread your prioritized goals and tasks until they *feel* right for you. Show them to no one. Make two sets of these 3" x 5" cards. One will be on your nightstand, another on your person. If you have an auto tape deck, make a tape of your own voice reading the goals and tasks.

Every morning, read the goals out loud. Clearly and precisely, visualize them, as if you already have realized them. Look at the tasks and feel yourself performing them. This process probably will take 15 minutes. Repeat it before you go to bed each night. If possible, try for one additional session in the middle of the day. In time, these goals and tasks will become a part of your life. You will know where you are, where you're going, and what there is to do. Review in the evening what you have accomplished that day and what you intend to accomplish the next day. Clearly and precisely, see yourself performing those tasks. Slowly, a new level of awareness will be realized, and you will see opportunities all around you that you never knew existed. Others will notice this change and be drawn like a magnet to your newfound strength.

Once each month, re-examine your goals and tasks. It is all right to add and modify goals, but, in most cases, I would caution against that. It is my experience that while successful people give careful thought to setting their directions, they are slow to change their minds. There is so much energy emanating from each of us. The successful person focuses most of it on the achievement of his/her goals. Unsuccessful people seem to set goals quickly (if they set them at all!) and change them often.

One final word of caution — do not set your goals too low. If you can, aim too high because, as you will discover later, you probably haven't aimed high enough.

Within a short time, you will find yourself highly motivated, relentlessly pursuing your goals and filled with a new sense of vigor and vitality.

In my many meetings, interviews, and close observations of successful and unsuccessful people, I have arrived at the following important conclusions:

- Successful people see life as a dynamic process that must be experienced in each moment of time.

- Outcomes are uncertain, but they believe that persistence and desire over time will help you to achieve the successful resolutions of your thoughts and dreams.

- Belief starts from within, at your very *core,* and works its way to the outside world. In other words, the world with all its benefits doesn't come to you — rather, you go out to the world and get what you want.

- A sense of who you are, and why you are where you are today in time and space, is important to success in life. Successful people are willing to deal with the pain this process involves.   It is the process that, in the final analysis, allows you to have a positive self-image that in turn opens a new and beautiful world to you.

- Successful people set goals, put their plans in writing, and monitor their performance. They rely minimally on the approval of others because they are both their own judges and critics. No one can be tougher; no one can be less fooled.

While I have tried to present a specific approach in this chapter, this is only my synopsis of 15 to 20 specific techniques. I have taken what I believe to be the best from each. My goal is to provide material that is immediately usable and not riddled with ambiguity. We know that goals alone will not change our life. As Kipling stated in his poem, *"If:"*

If you can dream and not make dreams your master,
If you can think and not make thoughts your aim,
If you can meet with triumph and disaster,
And treat those two imposters just the same.

In the final analysis, we must perform. Life feels wonderful when you are able to direct it in your own way, when you realize that your task is to discover the gifts you have, and then to develop what you need to give those gifts to the world. You will know you've cleared the first hurdle toward success when you feel like an integrated source of energy beaming toward self-realization. Words are inadequate to describe such a feeling, but you *will* know when it happens.

MONITORING PERFORMANCE

The techniques and concepts discussed earlier have provided us with goals and tasks. This section deals with monitoring performance. In discussing this problem with successful people, I discovered that, although the methods varied, they all had some form of a monitoring system. In the final analysis, however, I have concluded that there are two types of methods: in-place and portable.

If your work and personal routines are such that you spend a significant amount of time at the office and at home with minimal traveling, then I strongly suggest the in-place system. If, however, your daily routine is more random, involving lots of travel either in or out of town, then I suggest the portable system. Both systems will be supported by a daily review of your 3" x 5" cards. At a minimum, the cards should be reviewed every morning and before going to bed. If possible, try to work in a third session. Choose a place where you can be undisturbed for about 15 minutes. Read each goal, scan the tasks, then close your eyes and clearly visualize the goal as if you had already achieved it.

IN-PLACE CONTROL

In-place control consists of a large board that can be located in a den or other private area. If your living quarters cannot accommodate a private area, find some way to remove or cover the board when it is not in use. Most people using this system prefer a simple corkboard. Put the goals, along with the next task to perform, on a 3" x 5" card and tack them to the corkboard, positioning the cards so that the relative ranking of each goal is quite evident. Remember, the card does not contain all the steps involved in achieving the specific goal, just the next step or steps if certain activities can be performed in parallel. The basic idea is to make a transition from goals and tasks to a specific activity that you can incorporate into your normal routine. A goal will never be met until you take the first step. Once that step is completed, write the next step, etc., until the goal is achieved. After a particular step is completed, it is common for the knowledge acquired to result in a modification of the tasks remaining to complete the goal. This is a normal and healthy process. You learn as you go along and generally increase your effectiveness in achieving goals.

Another important reason for not listing all the steps on the board is that they may appear overwhelming at first. Unsuccessful people often play the game of making the goal so awesome that they do not know where to begin. Successful people just begin. They take to heart the Chinese proverb that says, "a trip of a thousand miles begins with but a single step."

Look at these tasks and your time availability for the week, then:

- Block in time for your top four goals.

- Complete your normal work schedule.

- Fill in remaining time with the next task for the next highest-ranking goal.

- Continue to assign tasks using the next highest ranked goal until the available time is consumed.

Do not assign too many tasks. It is important in the early stages that you complete some tasks and that you feel like you are moving toward achieving some of the goals. Visit the corkboard and interrogate yourself at least once a day. Soon you will get an idea of your capacity and comfort zone for handling projects.   In my conversations and research with successful people, it appears that they can be comfortable having anywhere from 24 to 48 projects in process at one time. This may sound like a lot of activity, but you will find it really isn't.

In time, your goals and tasks will become a part of you, and opportunities to achieve will surround you. Let me give you some examples of the dynamics involved in meeting your goals in this manner:

- The act of selectively sharing some of your goals with certain people who can help you is the equivalent of sowing seeds. Plant enough and, under the right conditions, they will sprout.

- A friend tells you of a new customer that he services who is growing at a rapid rate. You press further and learn that a favorable acquisition is rumored. You check out their 10K report, find the downside risk is reasonable, and invest in their stock.

- You find out at lunch that a business acquaintance you respect has lost his job. He would be an ideal partner in your new consulting firm. You contact him, and put the deal together.

- You read the newspaper and realize that the poor economy is creating many foreclosures. You decide that reading a book or pamphlet about how to save your home or real estate investment would be appropriate.

- You discover a new friend has lost his job and make a special effort to help him obtain interviews using your contacts. The friendship is greatly strengthened.

- You read a magazine article about transcendental

meditation that appeals to you. You locate where it is taught, sign up, and begin a daily program of meditation.

The examples are endless, but I believe you get the idea, and you can begin to understand why certain people are successful.

PORTABLE CONTROL

I personally use a portable system because I seem to be moving constantly from one place to the next. You can design or acquire commercially produced project cards and holders. The idea is similar to the in-place control. Because the systems usually have room for up to 100 projects, the idea is to have a card for each one. As progress is made in completing a task, record the facts on the card until the task is completed. Then discard the card or, if you are somewhat of a squirrel, store the card in a remote location. Office supply stores sell loose-leaf binder pockets that work well for this purpose. I carry the book with me and scan it at least once a day to make certain that I'm on course. I also find it useful to keep my date book, telephone book, a small calculator, and a pen in the sample packet. These days, it can all be stored in a palm-size computer.

In time, you will find the method that works best for you. It is not the technique that counts, but your discipline and belief in yourself. It is also the expectation that you can and will achieve the goals that you have identified as necessary to fulfill yourself. Let nothing or no one stand in your way. Unless you feel the resulting positive energy flowing in the right direction, you will be unhappy. Those who care about you want you to be happy. Rather than impeding your growth, they will foster it. Those who are jealous, demeaning, and pessimistic are harming your very soul. Consider whether they add to the quality of your life. You must love, nurture and care about yourself. Only then can your relationships be based on want, rather than need. When that strength surges through your being, you will know it, and so will others. As if you were a magnetic force, they will strive to be near you.

Chapter 3

The
Corporate
Clock

In a study of over one thousand companies that we have assisted, my company, Kibel Green Issa Inc. has concluded that the maintenance of organization **health** is a dynamic process requiring constant attention. A leader cannot merely set up the structure of a company and forget about it because it will not run by itself. In the United States, the vast majority of organizations fail. If we could uncover the secret of long-term success, we could unlock the door to enormous economic expansion by redirecting all of the resources currently devoted either to trying to save or to closing down failing companies.

OVERVIEW

Let's begin by asking ourselves "WHAT TIME IS IT?" at your company. Organizations with long-term **health** ask this continuously. To answer the question, I will introduce the concept of the **Corporate Clock** and explain how to tell time on it. THE ACTIONS YOU MUST TAKE TO RESTORE

HEALTH ARE A DIRECT RESPONSE TO YOUR POSI-
TION ON THE **CLOCK**. Shown below are the elements of
the **Corporate Clock**:

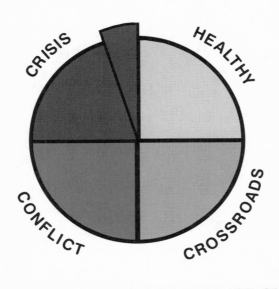

WHERE ARE YOU ON THE CORPORATE CLOCK?

The following short test will help you evaluate where your
company is on this **Clock**. The 22 key questions enumerated
here have been excerpted from a more comprehensive questionnaire that Kibel Green Issa Inc. uses in performing this
analysis for our clients.

1. Are there less than five layers of management from the
   top to the bottom of your organization?

2. Does the top executive have an *open door policy?*

3. Does the company perform annual Strategic and
   Contingency Planning involving all key decision-
   makers? Is the company actually managed by the Plan?

4. Is there a consistent compensation system? Do most executives consider the system fair?

5. Are the responsibilities given the executives matched by the authority to carry them out?

6. Does the formal organization chart follow the informal organization structure?

7. Is there a shared corporate vision at all levels in the organization?

8. Are the net profits as a percent of sales higher than those of the top companies in your industry?

9. Are gross profits in the top 10% of the industry?

10. Are accurate financial reports available before the 15th of the following month?

11. If the reports show poor performance, do they also indicate the action you must take to correct the problem?

12. When action is taken, do the reports reflect the impact of that action on the financial statements?

13. Is there an integrated advertising, sales and marketing program?

14. Is there a Personnel Manual, Sales Manual, and Summary of Financial Policies and Procedures?

15. Does the company have excellent relationships with employees, vendors, customers, shareholders, lenders, and regulatory agencies?

16. Is pricing tied to cost as well as to competitive requirements?

17. Has the company been free of major lawsuits?

18. Is there an organized program to connect top executives with:

    • the top decision-makers in the lender organization;

    • the top ten vendors; and

    • the top ten customers?

19. Are the average receivables under 60 days old?

20. Is employee turnover below 15% per year?

21. Are all of the key executive positions filled with talent that you would rate in the upper 20 percentile of their field?

22. Have acceptable phase one reports been received for all properties owned? If remediation is required, has the program been implemented, and have the related costs been built into the budget?

If the answer to any of these 22 questions is NO, then your company is probably not in the **Healthy** quadrant.

While exact determination cannot be made until you read and understand this book in its entirety, here are some preliminary guidelines:

• **Healthy** — All YES answers.

• **Crossroads** — One to Five NO answers.

- **Conflict** — Six to Ten NO answers.

- **Crisis** — Over Ten NO answers.

- **Red Zone** — Over Ten NO answers, plus a negative working capital with a deficit net worth.

In general, if your current ratio is less than 1.5 and/or your debt to equity ratio is greater than 2.0, you may not be **Healthy** even if you answered **YES** to all 22 questions. I must admit, however, that I do not know of any company that has answered yes to all questions and still had weak financials. Finally, if you have a negative working capital (current ratio under 1.0) and/or a deficit tangible net worth, you are in a **crisis** irrespective of the answers to the questions.

So, where are you on this **Corporate Clock?** Do you rate your organization higher or lower than the test results indicate? We usually find that owner/entrepreneurial executives tend to be optimistic and are unhappy with the test scores, while professional executives tend to be more realistic.

HOW DO CORPORATE CLOCKS WORK?

If I could work with an inventor and design **Corporate Clocks** for sale, business and professional people would build a pathway to my door. The **clocks** demonstrate that time accelerates as companies deteriorate. TIME IN THE **CRISIS** ZONE MOVES THIRTY TIMES FASTER THAN IN THE **HEALTHY** ZONE. In the **Healthy** quadrant, everything is in control and going well. There is plenty of time to correct any future problems that might occur. In addition, in the **Healthy** phase, the company has developed Strategic and Contingency Plans, and so is better prepared for emergencies. There is, in effect, an upward spiral. The company in the **Healthy** zone has more time, more resources, and more awareness, while the company in the **Crisis** zone has little time, limited resources, and no awareness. The company in the **Healthy** zone is able to work with *monthly* Cash Flow, Balance Sheet, and Profit and Loss information to maintain control. The information is timely and meaningful so that corrective action is being taken continuously to avoid drifting into the **Crossroads** zone. The company in the **Crisis** zone must work with *daily* Cash Flows and daily information related to all critical assets such as Inventories, Accounts Receivable, and Accounts Payable. The information is generally late. Corrective action usually is not taken because it is difficult to determine, through the information system, where the problem exists.

THE HEALTHY ZONE

In the **Healthy** zone, the Balance Sheet and the Profit and Loss Statement are really one statement. Executives understand that the Profit and Loss Statement merely explains the changes in the retained earnings portion of the Balance Sheet. Companies that stay in this zone understand that good **health** involves managing profits while keeping expansion at levels that the Balance Sheet can absorb. **Healthy** zone leaders recognize that, while leveraging a company can be a great way to maximize returns, it also can be the *kiss of death* when the economy turns south. The poor performance of many leveraged buyouts during the most recent recession illustrates my point. Executives of companies that remain in the **Healthy** zone for long periods of time recognize that, in the past 130 years, we have had recessions every 4.3 years. In a capitalist society, there will always be imbalances reflected as shortages in certain periods and excess capacity at other times. The **Healthy** company does the following:

• enjoys growth during the expansion phase but always

makes certain that the business can absorb at least a 30% decline in revenue;

• recognizes that it must raise equity, not debt dollars, if the business wishes to expand beyond its Balance Sheet capacity because it is in a rapidly growing market; and

• uses its superior financial position to acquire undervalued assets and businesses when the market is down.

Unfortunately, most companies try to maximize profits during the expansion phase, ignore the 30% downside rule, and fail when the market is down, all the while blaming their problems on the poor economy.

We see immediately that the company in the **Healthy** zone has more time to reflect than the company in **Crisis** or, for that matter, in any other zone. Therefore, they have the luxury of looking ahead and making certain that their business is running well today and also is prepared for the changes that will come tomorrow.

Even **Healthy** companies drift into the **Crossroads** zone at times. It is hard to always stay **Healthy**. However, since they are constantly monitoring their **health**, they inevitably recognize problems in early stages and correct them. The leaders always have their *hands on the steering wheel.*

THE CROSSROADS ZONE

Companies that move into the **Crossroads** zone and, invariably, into **Conflict** and on to **Crisis** probably were never **Healthy** in the first place. They experienced excellent profits and financial performance because they picked a business that was in the expansion phase. Margins were good, and inefficiency could be passed on in the form of increased prices.

Law firms provide an interesting example of this phenomenon. Throughout the heyday of the '80s, many of them were run quite inefficiently. Their administrative costs grew completely out of line, but they were able to pass these on in the form of ever-higher billing rates. Today, law firms are in better control. There is more competition, and rate increases are more difficult to implement. Those who survive now will be forced to examine their administrative costs and initiate breakthrough reductions. These law firms were never **Healthy**, but as long as they were enjoying the expansion phase, their weaknesses were masked.

The drift into the **Crossroads** zone is gradual. Many warning signals along the way have been ignored. Why don't all organizations correct their problems and return to **Healthy**? Here are some of the obstacles we have uncovered in our research:

- **Executive Denial** — They can't believe they have anything to do with the problem(s).

- **Executive Fear** — They feel that acknowledging an important problem reflects on their ability to manage and may result in a loss of prestige or position.

- **Executive Ignorance** — The information system simply does not tell them that a problem is occurring until it is too late.

- **Executive Absence** — Because things have been good, the owner or executive takes more time off, takes his/her *hands off the steering wheel,* and leaves the running of the business to bureaucrats.

In the **Crossroads** zone, time has accelerated. On the average, it is moving twice as fast as when the company was **Healthy**. Management needs not only monthly data but certain information on a bimonthly and, sometimes, weekly basis. The system must be interrogated more frequently. Solutions must be developed and implemented in a reasonable period of time. Since there are resources to make the corrections, time is still on the side of management.

THE CONFLICT ZONE

Ignoring the warning signs of the **Crossroads** zone will lead a company into the **Conflict** zone of the **Clock**. The problems now become overt. They can no longer be hidden. Time is moving six times faster than for a **Healthy** company and three times faster than for a company in **Crossroads**. Important people are leaving what they perceive to be a sinking ship. Resources have diminished and time is beginning to run out. Yet, action can be taken to move the company into a healthier position. Why doesn't it happen? Don't the executives want the company to survive? Here are some of the obstacles, in addition to those attributed to the drift into the **Crossroads** quadrant.

- **Lack Of Balance Sheet Knowledge** — Failure to focus on the management of assets and liabilities. The top executive does not understand the deterioration of the Balance Sheet.

- **Insensitivity To The Secured Lender** — Failure to realize that the bank lines of credit are at risk.

- **Taking Personnel For Granted** — Failure to recognize that the interests of employees are sometimes different from those of top management. Unless they are fiercely loyal, the most competent people will leave, further limiting the ability to identify and solve problems.

- **Executive Isolation** — Letting your people know that you do not take kindly to negative information. Therefore, none will be fed to you, even *while Rome is burning.*

- **Lack Of Planning** — Addressing problems as they come along. Everyone is in the fire fighting business, but no one knows where the fire is. There is no plan to deal with contingencies. When problems occur, everyone is under too much stress or in too much denial to do anything about them.

THE CRISIS ZONE

The **Crisis** zone is, of course, the most dangerous. Time is running out. It is moving at a pace thirty times that of the **Healthy** quadrant and five times that of the **Conflict** zone. Many companies have felt the sting of this zone. It has no respect for size or longevity. It reminds us that all companies are, in a sense, mortal. A few examples that corroborate my point are NASA, Chrysler, Texaco, Pan Am, Leaventhal and Horwith, Executive Life, and Johns Manville. Even IBM, considered immortal at one time, is having severe problems. This zone will be discussed in greater detail later in this chapter.

This, in essence, is our **Clock**. Understanding it can insure long-term success. Failure to understand its purpose may mean that, in the final analysis, your business will fail. Nothing goes on forever. Most businesses are recreated every five years. I hope that yours is one of them.

LEADERSHIP

Leadership is a dynamic process. In a rapidly changing

world, there is an on going need for a *rainmaker* to continuously reassess the economic and competitive environment. *Looking into the crystal ball* is not a task that can be delegated easily to other people. The world continues to grow more complex. At one time, it was only necessary to worry about your local region. Then it became necessary to look at the whole country. Soon, even mid-sized companies will have to consider the whole world. Technological improvements in the manufacturing, distribution, and control of products, services, and information continue to expand the geographic horizon, making distance less and less of a handicap. The rate of change is rapid, and motivated leadership must remain alert. For some leaders, the greatest enemy is their own success. They begin to believe their own press releases, forgetting they paid a public relations firm to prepare them! When this happens, they take their *hands off the steering wheel,* and their companies begin to drift toward the **Crossroads, Conflict,** and **Crisis** zones. Owners and key executives of businesses today cannot *let go.* The next level of management may not have the knowledge or the power to change that direction in sufficient time to prevent disaster. The larger the company, the longer the lead-time required to make adjustments. The sad news is that, no matter how good a business is today, it can no longer rest on its laurels and rely upon continued good fortune. *Rainmakers* who feel that they no longer have the energy for this task have the following choices:

• Get out;

• Sell;

• Get back in with both feet; or

• Find another *rainmaker.*

"Easier said than done!" I can hear you say. "I don't want

to get out!" "I don't want to get rid of my baby!" "I don't want to work that hard!" "I couldn't stand another person like me!" These statements, whether expressed or floating around inside your head, are the *kiss of death*. These are the reasons for scores of failures.

Many of our clients experienced success for a period of five years or longer, but forgot that the reason for their success was their personal involvement and attention to the business and their industry. The secret is in delegating everything but the rainmaking functions.

We have discovered another characteristic of **Healthy** companies. EXECUTIVES FIGHT ALL THE TIME, and THEY RARELY OPERATE IN A DEMOCRATIC MANNER. However, **Healthy** fighting focuses on business, not personal issues. It is **Healthy** for the Chief Financial Officer to irritate many people as he or she tries to cut costs and present a more conservative position on a given issue. The good CEO wants to hear all points of view and wants each executive to feel free to express a contrary opinion without fear of reprisal, so that the best decision can be made. It is one thing to point out to the Vice President of Manufacturing that his or her performance is poor, and to make constructive suggestions. It is quite another thing to say you don't like his or her attitude.

In a similar manner, executives often attend seminars (which tends to create tension because subordinates fear he or she will return with some crazy idea, and he or she rarely disappoints them!). They learn that true democracy is the answer to the company's problem(s). **Involve everyone in the decision making process, and your organization will improve overnight.** The problem is that most executives, though they deny it, are autocrats! This hypothetical will prove my point. What if one of your groups comes to a conclusion that you believe would be bad for your business? Would you implement it just to show that you are a good democrat? Funny, but I never get challenged about autocracy after that. So, now that we have established that you are an autocrat, let's make you a GOOD AUTOCRAT. Good autocrats have an *open door policy*. They *don't shoot the messenger*. They're fair, and they care about people, BUT THEY MAKE THE FINAL DECISION.

WHY KNOW THE CLOCK?

Now that you understand, on a macro basis, *how* the **Clock** works, let me briefly address *why* it is important to know where you stand. This is not just an intellectual exercise designed to satisfy curiosity. It is essential to long-term survival. The art of determining where you are on the **Clock** is, in and of itself, a call to arms. It is an *early warning system*. It tells you what is wrong and which problems need to be resolved. Your position on the **Clock** also tells you how much time is available before you enter the danger zone, guides you in selecting the *appropriate action* for solving any given problem, and gives you sufficient lead time to make the necessary corrections.

If, for example, you lost some key executives while in the **Healthy** zone, the *appropriate action* would be to examine your human resources and personnel functions, conduct exit interviews to better understand these losses, implement an executive search for replacements and, possibly, reorganize. If you are in the **Crisis** zone, there is not enough time to locate replacements. The *appropriate action* would normally be locating professional interim management and reshuffling existing executive responsibilities to get the job done. It may even require providing special financial incentives to the talented people that you must retain.

Or, if you have just drifted into the **Crossroads** zone and your inventory levels are too high, the *appropriate action* would be improving your inventory management system and possibly reorganizing that function to give it greater focus. If, however, this happens when you are in the **Crisis** zone, there is not enough time for improving the information system. The *appropriate action* would be slashing the inventory as quickly as possible (converting those assets into cash), and possibly taking a "write down" on the Profit and Loss Statement.

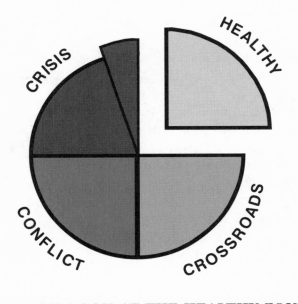

AN IN-DEPTH LOOK AT THE HEALTHY ZONE

Healthy organizations have strong Balance Sheets, Profits, and Cash Flow, not only in an absolute sense but also in relation to their competition. In comparison to any of their competitors, their gross profits are highest, their selling and G&A lowest. They have high levels of working capital and a debt structure that is not over-leveraged. This, however, is not enough. A company can be *lucky* for a period of time and ride the crest of an expanding market without having a clue about why their short-term financial performance is good. Most companies that think they are **Healthy** are merely *lucky*.

Chrysler performed well in producing large cars but did not accurately anticipate the impact of small Japanese cars on their market.   IBM did not judge, in time, the impact of Personal Computers on the sales of mainframe computers. Neither did they realize that their hardware was slowly becoming a commodity, nor that their future success would rely upon engineering software programs.   Many companies are now facing major lawsuits because they did not understand the changing litigation environment.   It is estimated that the sum total of knowledge doubles every five years.   The accuracy of this number is less important than the emphasis it places on the rapid rate of change in the modern world. Organizations that can't keep up will fail.

Truly **Healthy** companies have timely, meaningful management information systems. Strategic and Contingency Planning are part of their culture. They can live with monthly information because they are in control, understand where they have been, and know where they are going. They are always looking ahead, always anticipating the future, and always making certain they can deal with it. They recognize that, in a capitalist system, there will always be expansion, recession, and stagnation periods, and they are prepared for them.   They are always changing organization structure to meet the needs of the market, recognizing that an organization must be fluid and dynamic for long-term survival. Talent runs high at all levels, and executives are compensated based on performance, not on seniority or type of skill. They have strong ties to customers and vendors, especially those who sell them money — the financial institutions. They maintain contact with the capital markets at all times. They are structured to move rapidly when a change is required. Unless all of this is in place, an organization is not **Healthy**.

The overweight individual who doesn't exercise and survives on a diet filled with fried foods may pass his/her next physical, but the long-term prognosis is not good. What matters is not simply getting a good report card today, but making certain you discipline yourself to insure that all future report cards also will be excellent.

BLUEPRINT FOR SUCCESS

After almost twenty years of research, Kibel Green Issa Inc. has developed a model for the structure needed to insure ongoing corporate **health**. We know that eight out of ten businesses in the United States ultimately fail. What is it, we asked, that the other two of ten do that is different? We discovered there is a pattern. We discovered that the 20% of companies who exhibit long-term **health** concentrate, either formally or informally, on three interactive systems that are monitored and updated continuously, while the other 80% do not.

- **System One** — Monitoring the status of the company on the **Corporate Clock** by means of an annual **health** check and identifying the projects necessary to return to **health**.

- **System Two** — Engaging in annual Strategic and Contingency Planning. This planning cycle becomes part of the company's culture and is not performed merely for the sake of producing an impressive manual. The organization *lives the Plan.*

- **System Three** — Utilizing the management information system to identify ongoing problem areas and opportunities so they can be addressed promptly.

How does each system get implemented?

- **System One** — The question that must be answered each year is *"What time is it at your company?"* [Our firm uses a

49-page Operations Review (**health** check) Questionnaire to determine the answer to that question.]

1. A precise assessment of whether you are **Healthy** or at a **Crossroads**, **Conflict** or **Crisis** stage.

2. An identification of the projects that must be completed to return to **health**. These projects not only restore **health** but also, in the short run, result in significant savings.

- **System Two** — We recommend that your company initiate an off-site Strategic and Contingency Planning session. The output will include at a minimum:

1. Mission Statement;

2. Analysis of Strengths and Weaknesses;

3. Contingency Planning;

4. Goals and Objectives;

5. Strategies; and

6. Tactics with assigned responsibilities.

After the Plan is developed, it must become a working document throughout the year.

- **System Three** — Along with the expansion of technology, an explosion of information from the financial and data processing departments has evolved. Usually there is too much information and often it is not in a form, that is useful for decision-making. The company must conduct a review of all reports and documents with the personnel who actually use them to determine what they need to run their departments. Generally, the result is a streamlining of the system, which evokes smiles on the faces of the department heads because the reports will be written in their language.

Staying **Healthy** is hard work, but without the right diet, stress control and exercise program, maximum effort can fail to produce even minimal results.

Let us now look at some of the important elements of good **health** in greater detail. They are:

- Management by a *rainmaker;*

- Accurate and timely management information;

- Strategic and Contingency Planning;

- Dynamic organization structure;

- Compensation based on performance;

- Strong ties to customers and vendors;

- Strong ties to financial institutions;

- An ongoing understanding of the capital markets;

- Ongoing **health** checks;

- An understanding of the Balance Sheet;

- *Open door policy* at the top; and

- A general reluctance to sign guarantees of any sort.

ACCURATE AND TIMELY MANAGEMENT INFORMATION

The following simple test will help you see if your organization has accurate and timely information:

1. Do you have significant end-of-the-year adjustments or surprises after the outside accountants have analyzed the books?

2. When performance is poor in a given month, does the information system indicate what is wrong and what action you must take?

3. When you have taken that action, does the information system reflect that the action was correct and produced the desired result?

4. Do you receive the information before the fifteenth of the following month?

5. Finally, do you have confidence in the accuracy of the data, or do executives fight over its meaning?   If the answer is **NO** to any of these questions, then your information system is **NOT HEALTHY**.

Having to make adjustments at the end of the year means that the information you have been analyzing throughout the year has been inaccurate. Errors in inventory are a sign of a poorly designed cost accounting system. Private companies often hide behind the logic that losses are good because they reduce taxes. However, these losses also are telling you that real profits are declining. In the long run, this will be reflected as reduced cash flow.

Oftentimes, information systems are nothing more than

accounting reports which provide the Balance Sheet, Profit and Loss Statement and Cash Flow information in a form that is not usable for executive decision-making. The information system must report in a language that the sales, operating, and financial executives can understand. If the financial officer has to explain the meaning of the report, something is wrong. Is the information broken down by product line or by type of service? Can each function or department be measured? Are controllable costs segregated from uncontrollable costs? Does management understand, in the final analysis, that **ALL COSTS ARE CONTROLLABLE** at some level, and that each cost must be under the control of a responsible executive? Otherwise, how can you hold anyone responsible for corrective action? Sometimes, we are told that costs such as rent and equipment depreciation are uncontrollable. These costs, however, were incurred because some key executive made a decision to lease, buy, or build a plant of a given size in a given location. Other executives selected the type of equipment. I have had clients in comparable businesses with similar sales volumes. Company A utilized twice as many square feet as Company B, yet Company A thought they were efficient.

In most businesses, a poor month calls for a top executive meeting at which everyone tries to *guess* what went wrong. The problem is often blamed on reduced volume with no one taking responsibility for reducing variable costs in a timely manner. Research projects must be initiated to find out what happened because the information system obviously is inadequate.

Finally, decisions are made and action is taken because management feels it must always take action. But did the action result in a correction of the problem? If we don't fully understand the problem in the first place, and if we don't know who is responsible, how can we be sure that the correct executive is taking the correct action? If the system does not measure performance tied to responsibility, how do we know that the action solved the problem? Next month might be better, but for reasons independent of the actions taken.

STRATEGIC AND CONTINGENCY PLANNING

Many executives ask me "What do I need strategic planning for?" and are afraid that "Contingency Planning will just make my people nervous." My response is that almost **ALL** of the companies that have remained in the **Healthy** zone through more than one recessionary cycle included Strategic and Contingency Planning in their corporate culture, and **NONE** of the companies that were in a **Crisis** did any of this type of planning. The evidence is overwhelming! Why this occurs should be obvious.

Strategic Planning always keeps your organization looking ahead. In deciding what your corporate mission is, identifying your strengths and weaknesses, understanding your competition, setting goals and objectives, developing tactics and a supportive follow-up system, you and your key people are forced to pay attention to the future. You may or may not be doing well today, but you must be on the lookout for obstacles related to tomorrow. Can government legislation hurt you? Have new, more aggressive and creative competitors appeared on the scene? Is your product or service on the verge of becoming obsolete? Are you too expensive? Is your management talent limited? These are the kinds of questions you must wrestle with each time you do Strategic Planning.

Planning must be part of the corporate culture. Many companies go through the motions of Strategic Planning and create an impressive manual. A copy of this manual is given to all participating executives. Invariably, it sits in a dominant location in their offices, never to be read again. Management then returns to the old habits they followed before the Plan was developed. When the Plan is part of the company's culture, however, **THE COMPANY IS RUN BY THE**

PLAN. All key executives are involved in its creation. They have bought into it and see themselves as an integral part of its success. There is a spirit of working together toward a shared vision, creating a synergy inside the organization that is highly focused, rather than diffused. It is hard to compete with a company that is currently doing well, knows why, and has a shared vision about where it is going.

Contingency Planning is another practice that is often avoided because it is not consistent with an executive's or owner's optimistic nature. "Why talk about problems and make people nervous?" he/she will say. "How can I tell an executive that his or her job will be on the line if revenue declines below a certain level?"

Let us deal with each issue separately. I generally suggest that a Contingency Plan be based on a 30% reduction in revenue. The challenge is to keep the company viable under those conditions. This would involve reducing space, the size of the executive group, the number of support personnel and so on. In a **Crisis**, with time accelerating at thirty times the pace of **Healthy**, do you really want to spend your time figuring out what to do, or would you rather be implementing a carefully thought out Contingency Plan which was developed in a relaxed environment? Think how optimistic you will feel when you know you can survive even under negative circumstances. After all, the economy and your business follow a cyclical pattern. The secrets of long-term survival are (1) to remain viable during bad times, and (2) to be in a position to take advantage of a down market by acquiring your competition or entering new businesses when there is little downside risk. The only people who will be nervous will be those executives at risk if business falls off. It is for this reason that outside advisors are often used in Contingency Planning. The Plan does not have to be shared with everyone.

Contingency Planning introduces you to the Balance Sheet. The report that you tended to ignore as long as profits were up now looms in importance. In fact, it is the Balance Sheet that determines how fast you can grow without risking failure in your downside Plan. The primary reason why companies so often fail relates to the business cycle. When the cycle is in its expansionary phase, the business is leveraged. In the short term, this may maximize profits. Unfortunately, it is also the fastest way to accelerate the downward cycle when the economy turns in the opposite direction.

It is in this way that the Contingency and Strategic Plans are connected. The Contingency Plan will set a limit on your ability to grow without injecting equity into the business. If the additional equity comes from your personal resources, then more of your capital is at risk. If the additional equity comes from outside sources, then you have to be mentally prepared to give up partial interest in the business and recognize that there will be a partner looking over your shoulder.

"Am I not giving up profits in the boom period when I follow this procedure?" you may ask. Possibly, but you will survive the down turn and be around to enjoy the future booms. There is, however, an even greater gift. During those down turns when many of your competitors are suffering, you will be in a position to make acquisitions, at bargain rates, which will more than compensate you for your supposed lost profits.

Strategic and Contingency Planning is what successful business people do — whether formally, or informally. As long as we live in a capitalistic society where we will experience business cycles and competition, the winners will be the planners.

DYNAMIC ORGANIZATION STRUCTURE

Top executives are often proud of their organization charts. The neatly drawn boxes show you the reporting relationship of each key individual. Sometimes there are even written job descriptions that spell out the role, responsibility, and authority of each position. The material can be quite impressive, but it can also be very misleading.

First of all, the formal charts may not reflect the way the organization really works (which is all that really matters). Second, even if the chart does reflect the true picture, it may not be appropriate for effective decision-making.

Organization charts are not static. They should be changed as often as necessary to address the needs of the marketplace. Executives should not get hung up on titles. Businesses should be kept as flat as practical so that communication errors are minimized and decisions are made close to the source. Companies as large as IBM have been working on reducing the number of layers of management. The greater the number of layers, the longer it takes for information to get to the decision-makers and the more likely the information will be distorted when it gets there. Also, there is some certainty that the decision-maker will be too far removed to make an informed decision. He is, therefore, dependent on advice from subordinates (who often have their own agendas).

For a long time, the technical professionals in the automobile industry knew that the Japanese were producing quality cars. Why were their companies so slow to react? Why didn't companies like IBM see the changing requirements related to mainframe computers? These organizations are filled with gifted executives, but something in the structure for communicating and transmitting fell apart. Often, in a fluid organization, executives are pulled from different departments to address a problem. They are allowed to cross over jurisdictional lines. They bypass the usual up and across pattern required to deliver information without disturbing anyone's *fiefdom*. The individuals who possess the knowledge have direct communication with those individuals who make decisions without heavy staff intervention.

In dynamic organizations, corporate staffs are amazingly small because most decisions are made on a decentralized basis. The top executives want to minimize the use of middlemen in the information and decision-making process.

The danger of overly formalizing charts and job descriptions is that they remain static. Individuals begin to have a vested interest in the structure and have difficulty making changes. In a dynamic organization, the structure is fluid and subject to change. There are few *turfs* because there is a shared common vision and recognition that a synergistic approach becomes a win-win situation for everyone involved.

COMPENSATION BASED ON PERFORMANCE

Most studies have shown that employees are more concerned about the *fairness* of their compensation in relation to other employees than they are about the relationship between their compensation and the marketplace.

This probably occurs because it is difficult to assess market value. Relative compensation is easier to measure. Employees tend to look at the issue of fairness by comparing the contribution they make to the well being of the organization in relation to the contribution of others. Employers, unfortunately, tend to compensate based on position, education, title and seniority. These factors often do not relate to real contribution and, therefore, disturb the employee's sense of fairness. Employers too often tend to reward *squeaky wheels*. The individuals who fail to *toot their own horn* are often forgotten until the day they resign. Then everyone realizes how difficult life has become now that they've gone. The brilliant Secretary who continuously saves the day for the President may be more valuable than a Controller who is just a *bean counter*. The Foreman in the warehouse who knows where every product is located may be more valuable than the new MBA who, while bright, may be making little contribution.

It is easier to avoid merit and rely on objective approaches such as seniority, education and title. The major problem with this approach is that the *best and the brightest* want to be measured by merit, and the *dead wood* would prefer compensation based on seniority. One has to look no further than at government to see how well the seniority system works.

Merit requires the company to have a good information system by which individual and group performance can be measured. The information in that system must be accurate and accepted by the employees as reasonable criteria for measurement of their performance.

Competent employees know they are competent, and *dead wood* employees know they are *dead wood*. Competent employees also know who the *dead wood* employees are, and *dead wood* employees reluctantly acknowledge who the competent ones are. If a system is not based on merit, and the best people do not see the economic benefit of superior performance, they will either leave the organization, significantly reduce their efforts, or begin to *bad mouth* the management of the company, spreading a cancer throughout the organization.

Companies with long-term **health** reward employees based on performance and are very sensitive to fairness issues between employees. They also cull out the *dead wood* as soon as they are identified.

STRONG TIES TO CUSTOMERS AND VENDORS

A chain of hardware stores in deep financial trouble was working with a somewhat uncooperative financial institution. Their only hope was to get very generous terms from the vendors. There was no real business reason the vendors should offer the 120-day terms they required except that the owners, who had been in business for many decades, had cultivated close relationships with the decision-makers in their vendor organizations. It was because of their relationships that they received the generous credit they required. The company was ultimately saved, is still in business (doing well), and remains loyal to its vendors to this day.

I can tell you many stories of organizations in **Crisis** who were saved because of strong vendor ties and those brought to the brink of failure because they ignored or had poor vendor relations.

When business is good and your organization is very profitable, it is common to ignore the vendors. After all, at that time, they need you and not the other way around. I become more convinced as time passes that relationships are a key to long-term survival. I have seen organizations in the same business where Company A was weaker than Company B, yet Company A survived while Company B failed because of its inability to get cooperation from its vendors.

I strongly suggest to our clients that they take out their date books, list their top fifteen vendors, get the names of the decision-makers, and make appointments for lunch, golf, tennis, or the theater. Find out about these people (i.e., number of children, hobbies, life issues, etc.), *then* find a way to do them a favor within the next twelve months. In addition to having a loyal vendor, you will learn more about your company than your employees can ever tell you. How are you looked upon in the industry? What does your competition see your strengths and your weaknesses to be? Are your products or services becoming obsolete? Is quality and service slipping behind that of your competition? Do they feel you are about to be sold, or that you are in financial trouble? The decision-maker in the vendor organization sees you more as a peer than as a customer and has a selfish interest in seeing that you succeed. This is an important relationship to cultivate.

The same approach also should be used for the cultivation of your top fifteen customers. Who are they? Who are the decision-makers? Again, take out your date book and set up appointments with each of them. When the economy gets tough, they may choose to do business with you because of the relationship you have established. If the industry is going through changes, they could be your *early warning system*. They will be the first to let you know of problems in your organization.

Many top executives in our client organizations will say to me, "But we already do this. My Vice President of Purchasing (or Manufacturing) stays close to the vendors, and my Vice President of Sales and Marketing stays close to the customers." Unfortunately, that is not the same as the owner or top executive personally keeping in touch with the decision-makers.

If your vendor is a mid-sized company or smaller, you should meet with the owner or CEO. If your vendor is a major conglomerate, you should connect with the decision-maker for your account. Your personnel can meet with those who service your account. They are not usually the decision-makers.

This is particularly true in your customer organizations. The individual who purchases from your company should be treated well by your sales department, but the decision-maker should be treated well by you personally.

I am often told, "Look, I'm a busy guy and don't have time for that sort of stuff. That's why I have an organization under me!" I can only repeat that your very survival during down economic cycles may depend on that relationship. Are you in the habit of delegating away your very survival? In addition, as the *rainmaker* and visionary in your organization, wouldn't you want a direct *early warning system* so that you could change the strategic direction of your organization if that should become necessary? **About 30 percent of a top executive's time should be spent on relationships with vendors, customers, sources of capital, and on planning future direction.** The executives under you probably do a superb job of running their functional area, but they depend on you to preserve the company's long-term **health**. Don't let them down!

STRONG TIES TO FINANCIAL INSTITUTIONS

Think of the financial institution that supplies you with money as another vendor who sells you dollars rather than goods or services. These vendors have the ability to help you expand or to put you out of business. They are not partners in your business and, while they are pleased with your programs of growth and expansion, they are more pleased if you have a strong Balance Sheet and can pay back your debt. This relationship, which is so critical to the long-term **health** of your organization, is usually delegated to the Controller or Chief Financial Officer.

The account manager of the financial institution and your financial executive develop a working relationship. Neither of them has authority over your account. If you get into serious trouble, the account will be taken from the account manager and transferred to the Workout Department. The workout people have very little interest in your account manager who, if he is still with the financial institution, is trying to save his/her own reputation. Workout people may be less kind or understanding. Their job is to maximize the return to the bank or minimize the bank's losses. That is how they are measured. They are not focused on your economic survival unless it happens to coincide with the best interests of the bank.

Once there are problems, it is useless to try to establish a working relationship with the decision-maker at the financial institution. The time to develop that relationship is *now*, while you are **Healthy**.

You must identify the decision-maker. If your bank is small, that individual is probably the President. If it is a larger institution, that individual is most likely the head of the Loan Department. Get the person's name and personally contact him/her. Find out how many children they have, their spouse's name, hobbies, interests, etc., and keep the contact alive.

Many failures have been averted because of this type of relationship. When a business gets into trouble, the financial institution often blames the problem on lack of credibility, competence and, sometimes, honesty. Once started, these rumors make it very difficult to get any concessions from the lender. If, however, there is a good relationship at the top, it is unlikely these horrible traits will be attributed to your organization. You will be considered an ethical, competent executive who got caught in a bad economic climate and needs their support for a period of time.

Mr. X, an executive who ran a successful empire for over forty years, was in financial trouble. Most of the major banks in California were his lenders. If he was forced to liquidate, it was clear that there would not be enough to pay back all the debt. Technically, he was bankrupt. The bankers knew and respected this individual. He was always honest. He had turned over much of the business to a younger group of executives, and they leveraged it into the ground. Mr. X was in his seventies and no one wanted to see him *out on the street.* It was agreed to set aside a pool of money for him so that he could live with respect. We separately negotiated the allocation of assets between the other institutions. As time passed, we were also able to save the company, and the institution did not suffer any loss.

This could not have happened without the willingness on the part of the banks to wait and be cooperative. I contend that the personal relationship between Mr. X and the banks made the difference. Other companies with fewer problems but poor relationships with lenders, failed in the same time period. The message is simple. **You are responsible for the relationship with your financial institution.** Your Chief Financial Officer or Controller can certainly handle the day-to-day relationship, but that does not replace a close connection at the top.

The relationship is useful even if business is good. The

lender will be more inclined to increase your line of credit and provide special lending facilities to help you initiate new ventures. He/she also can introduce you to potential customers. Time spent cultivating these relationships is time well spent.

UNDERSTANDING THE PERCEIVED VALUE

The experienced executive understands that it is not only important to build a **Healthy** organization internally, but to be sensitive to perceived value. These ideas are a new world to many executives. How you position your company can have an enormous impact on its value in the marketplace. We recently completed a private placement for a major retailer. Based on conversations with some people on Wall Street, this retailer believed that his business could be sold for $90 million. When we were asked to look at the business, we realized that (1) operational improvements could be made to increase value; and (2) the story of the retailer's potential needed to be presented more forcefully. In the right hands, the company was worth substantially more than $90 million. Six months later, we sold the business for $135 million. Failure to understand the capital markets could have cost this retailer $45 million.

A high tech company with a deficit net worth and a negative working capital (technically bankrupt) was prepared to give up 25% of its net worth. The CEO needed to demonstrate the opportunity that could be created if capital were obtained. We developed a five-year Plan, brought it back to its present value, allowed for a discount and sold the 25% interest for $10 million. The uninitiated may have valued the business at less than zero. Raising money is an art, and if the owner of a **Healthy** company does not learn that art, he/she will be doomed to be a small time operator. Normally, capital is needed to grow and to create significant personal wealth.

UNDERSTANDING THE CAPITAL MARKETS

Equity capital may be raised by selling common stock: (1) to the public at large which, of course, makes it a public issue; or (2) to a select group of buyers, in which case it is referred to as a private placement. Furthermore, both public issues and private placements may be sold nationally (interstate) or limited to one state (intrastate). Public issues also can be divided into segments, with one segment sold in U.S. markets and another sold internationally. The first time a company sells stock to the public, the issue is called an initial public offering or IPO. The public market for trading common shares is called the secondary market.

The significance of these distinctions relates to regulatory requirements, cost, stock appreciation potential, flexibility, and market acceptance. Prior to developing specific Plans to sell common stock, companies must weigh each of these factors in light of capital needs, previous profitability, and management capabilities. As a start, it's necessary to determine precisely how much new capital is needed, the percentage of ownership current shareholders are willing to relinquish, and the uses to which the new capital will be applied.

Even if internal indicators point to an affirmative decision, the external timing for a stock issue may be way off. Time and again, companies begin to expedite a public offering only to learn, after spending thousands of dollars, that some uncontrollable circumstance prevents or delays completing the job. The main culprits responsible for killing plans for public offerings are the following:

• A national event;

• Stock market weakness;

- A stock market collapse;

- A rapid decline in an industry;

- Out-of-control inflation; and

- A hard recession (if the economic indicators continue trending downward).

Public stock offerings are very expensive and usually cannot be justified for total amounts of less than $5 million. To make an IPO cost effective, a company should be generating annual sales of at least $10 million, although this platform decreases for very high-growth industries. Issues of less than $7.5 million, defined as small issues by the Securities and Exchange Commission (SEC), will be less expensive than larger issues. Even then, issuing costs of $250,000 to $500,000 are the rule rather than the exception.

Once the issue is sold, ongoing administrative costs add significant overhead. Costs to produce periodic SEC reports and proxy statements, printing and mailing expenses, annual fees for accountants, lawyers, registrars, and transfer agents add up in a hurry. New shareholders also look for a return on their investment in the form of dividends. Since dividends are not deductible for tax purposes, after-tax dollar payments increase operating costs even more.

Other than cost, three potential problems must be addressed. First, SEC approval must be obtained before the stock can be sold. State securities commission approval is required for intrastate issues. Because market timing is frequently such a crucial ingredient, the actual issue date requires careful planning. More than one issue has failed because SEC or state commission approval took too long and the market window closed before the offering was ready. The decision to proceed in spite of such a delay is likely to result in a share price substantially lower than anticipated.

Second, even after the stock is sold, there is no assurance that active trading will follow. This can nullify incentive programs structured to reward management employees with non-cash stock options and make it difficult to use stock for business acquisitions.

A third problem has to do with a company's management. It doesn't take long to realize that the trading price of a company's shares relates directly to its earnings trend. Management personnel may spend more time worrying about increasing share earnings than they do about running the company efficiently.   Short-term decisions that favorably affect earnings for this quarter or this year may, in the long run, do more harm than good.

Probably the most aggravating going-public issue confronting private business owners is their loss of privacy. SEC regulations require complete disclosure of the most intimate and proprietary company matters: officers' compensation, personal histories, incentive programs, forecasts of future earnings, planned new-product developments, and strategic operating plans tend to be the most troublesome. Not only must this information be revealed in the offering, it also must be updated continually in quarterly and annual reports — all of which become public information.

Preparation for all of this usually begins at least three years in advance. Since there are significant costs, the advantages and disadvantages should be clearly understood. Here are a few of the major ones:

ADVANTAGES OF GOING PUBLIC

- **Financial Stability** — A public stock issue may be the only way to raise enough growth capital for third-stage internal expansion or business acquisitions.

- **Amount Of Capital Needed** — Going public rather

than through debt financing can raise greater amounts of capital.

- **Flexible Returns** — Equity capital does not require a fixed cash outlay on a predetermined schedule, such as interest and principal payments. Although shareholders will expect dividend returns, the company unilaterally determines the timing and amount of payments.

- **Ownership Control** — The market receives initial issues better in small segments. Owners of privately held companies can raise substantial equity capital without losing control. Secondary offerings that disperse ownership interest among hundreds or even thousands of shareholders can be structured to leave previous owners in effective control with less than 51 percent stock ownership.

- **Ready Exit** — Disposing of shares in a privately held company when it's time to retire or otherwise get out can be a sticky problem. With an established trading market, insiders have a ready means of disposing of their interests — subject, of course, to insider trading rules. Also, the market value of shares can be readily established for estate valuations.

- **Employee Incentives** — Stock options can provide a valuable incentive for key employees.

- **Improved Borrowing Capacity** — Banks and other financial institutions view additional equity infusions favorably, since cash balances are increased at the same time that debt/equity ratios improve.

- **Improved Company Image** — Most privately held companies have a difficult time establishing a profile in industries dominated by large public firms. The publicity that goes with a public offering can easily change that, increasing public visibility and thereby stimulating sales and attracting higher quality personnel.

- **Increased Personal Net Worth** — Nothing boosts personal net worth faster than establishing a market value for an owner's stock holdings.

DISADVANTAGES OF GOING PUBLIC

- **Ongoing Expense** — The ongoing expense after the stock begins trading can be a significant burden for smaller companies. A variety of reports — 10Ks, 8Ks, and 10Qs — must be filed regularly. Annual certified audits, added legal fees, printing expenses, and public relations costs are not essential for privately held companies. In addition, employees now must spend time complying with SEC and exchange regulations. Additional expense of $60,000 to $100,000 a year is not uncommon.

- **Closing Out Venture Capital** — Typically, venture capital firms get involved in financing privately held companies with the understanding that at a future date the company will go public. An IPO now closes this door.

- **Loss Of Management Flexibility** — Once a company has gone public, its management personnel lose flexibility for making decisions and developing Strategic Plans. Abiding by SEC disclosure regulations can preempt valuable competitive secrecy easily. Furthermore, some corporate strategies require shareholder approval, such as mergers, business acquisitions, new stock issues, and so on, prohibiting management personnel from making these decisions on their own.

- **Liability** — Officers and directors of public companies remain fully liable for any violations of SEC or exchange regulations.

- **Potential Loss Of Control** — Depending on the percentage of ownership in public hands, a Board of Directors' loss of control can be an onerous possibility. Many adversarial proxy fights have resulted in the dismissal of a company's original owners.

- **Company Skeletons** — Once a company issues public stock, its affairs — past, present, and future — become public knowledge. Bankruptcies, criminal records, lawsuits, and other potentially damaging events related to officers and directors must be disclosed in prospectuses and registrations.

- **Poor Economic Timing** — A company might expend a substantial amount of cash getting ready to go public only to learn that the market timing is off.

Just as it is important for the leaders of **Healthy** companies to understand accounting because it is the language of business, so must they understand the capital markets, which hold the key to significant wealth.

UNDERSTANDING THE BALANCE SHEET

I have always been somewhat critical of business schools and the financial community in general. There is often undue emphasis on the Profit and Loss Statement, earnings per share, revenue, expense budgets and the like. Yet, when a company gets into trouble, it dispenses with these statements in favor of the Balance Sheet. If a company is going to get out of a **Crisis**, it will happen through the careful management of assets and liabilities and the restructuring of assets and liabilities through renegotiation. Since this is always the case in a **Crisis,** you would think that it is important for a **Healthy** company also to pay attention to the report that is attached to the Profit and Loss Statement. Companies that remain **Healthy** over long periods of time appreciate the importance of the Balance Sheet. They recognize that, in a sense, we are reading only one financial statement. The Profit and Loss Statement merely explains the change in retained earnings on the Balance Sheet, just as the Cash Flow Statement explains how the asset "cash" either increased or decreased over a given time period.

First, there is a focus on the major assets. Cash is managed through a Cash Flow report that explains what happened to this all-important asset and what is forecast to happen in the future. Cash usually is obtained through collection of receivables, but also can come in through the sale of other assets, through borrowing or the raising of equity. The operating goal is to reduce the elapsed time of converting assets to cash. The typical process involves buying and storing inventory, which may or may not be converted and subsequently is sold. This, in turn, converts the inventory to a receivable, which becomes cash when collected. Manufacturing companies must convert the inventory before it can be sold. Hopefully, profit is produced in that process so that more inventory can be purchased, and investment can be made in fixed assets.

Good management, therefore, keeps tight control over collections to reduce the aging of the receivables and keeps its inventory to a minimum. It is sensitive to the concepts of *reduced cycle time* and *just in time* inventory control. Obsolete inventory and obsolete fixed assets are converted into cash as soon as possible because these managers realize that the passage of time results in reduced value.

Second, there is a focus on the major liabilities. Unsecured creditors are an excellent source of cash (zero percent interest!). Prompt payment of one's debts is not necessarily the best way to manage accounts payable. While a company wants to be reliable, it should extend payment terms whenever possible. Some of the best companies in the United States today are not necessarily fast payers, but they are reliable and honor their extended payment commitments. Secured creditors, on the other hand, are managed somewhat differently. Of course, the amount of debt should be minimized. While many companies play with the "float," this can be a dangerous game because overdrafts at the bank create serious problems. The bank will often interpret this behavior to mean financial trouble or, at a minimum, poor financial control. **Healthy** companies negotiate the best rate and terms. They understand when to use revolving lines, receivable and inventory lines, term loans, and the like.

Healthy companies, therefore, have excellent reports related to secured and unsecured liabilities. In fact, where there are significant contingent liabilities (which may not appear in the financial statements), these, too, are monitored.

A myriad of ratios that connect the Profit and Loss Statement to the Balance Sheet are all part of the information system **Healthy** companies receive along with the Profit and Loss reports. This information includes:

- accounts payable and receivables analysis;

- inventory turnover;

- debt to equity evaluation;

- current ratio and working capital analysis; and

- return on investment.

Balance Sheet knowledge is generally weak in companies in **Crisis** and is strong in companies with long-term **health**. What more can I say?

OPEN DOOR POLICY AT THE TOP

Most top executives like to tell me they have an *open door pol-icy* until I describe the nature of such a policy. For example, it does not mean that you keep your door open all the time or that top executives can meet with you anytime they feel it is important.   It means that **anyone, at any level in the organization, can see you, in confidence, without going through the chain of command.   Furthermore, they know that you will not use the information they share with you against them**. Ask yourself this question: "Is my entire understanding about how my business is doing based on the input received from my key executives, or do I also have other sources against which I can check this input?" Key executives have a way of sticking together and protecting each other. They will never tell you they are doing a poor job or that an employee revolt is in the making. They never will rec-ommend that they or their position be eliminated or consolidated.

Employees who are close to the action see problems and opportunities that no one else can see. They need access to you, particularly when they do not trust or have respect for their boss. These employees must be able to see you in confidence and pass on their observations without being told that they must go through the chain of command. That chain may apply to everyone else except the top executive. This is the only way you are going to know what is going on. Otherwise, you will be insulated from the truth forever.

Many years ago, I was running a public company. We had manufacturing facilities across the United States. One of our major facilities on the East Coast was performing badly, despite the fact that I had my most qualified Plant Manager in that position. The problem befuddled me until one day when one of the employees in our accounting department informed me that, every day at noon, my star manager would take off with his secretary and not return until the following day. Everyone but me knew about the problem. If not for the open door policy, I probably still would not know about the problem.

In another situation we lost a major customer. I could not understand why until I discovered that one of my key people was unwittingly dating the customer's girlfriend. After making modifications in his social life, and with some apologies, we got the account back.

The information described above cannot be obtained by reading the financial statements or chatting with your key executives. The *open door policy* must be combined with an *open mind policy*. Some executives make it clear to everyone that they do not want to hear bad news. This creates a second level of insulation. Your door may be *open,* but few will enter.

It requires great skill to honor confidence while utilizing information. As I have already mentioned, it is an art form worth learning. **Healthy** companies understand the power of this policy. Never let the chain of command get in the way of keeping fully informed.

RELUCTANCE TO SIGN PERSONAL GUARANTEES

This last element does not apply to major corporations since the magnitude of their debt is so large that a personal guarantee is meaningless. However, for many mid-sized and smaller corporations, financial institutions often require a personal guarantee. When your organization is weak, you have no choice but to sign the guarantee. However, when you are strong, **Healthy**, and considered to be well run with a bright future, there may be an opportunity to avoid the guarantee.

Financial institutions will always tell you that it is standard practice to sign a continuing guarantee. Nevertheless, many of our clients have been able to avoid this. When a company is in trouble and there is a personal guarantee, a corporate bankruptcy is often followed by a personal bankruptcy. Much of the debtor's negotiation leverage is gone when the debt is recourse. When your existing lender requires a personal guarantee and you have a strong financial statement, it is best to talk to other institutions. Psychologically, it is difficult for your existing lender to give up something they possess without receiving something in return. This is not a problem for the new lender. Sometimes you will be asked to pay a slightly higher rate. This should be given serious consideration. If the marketplace is resistant, you may want to think about placing a *cap* on the guarantee, leaving enough personal net worth so that you can go about your life if the business fails.

Another alternative is to make the guarantee conditional. Ask the lender why they want the guarantee in the first place. They may tell you that "the current ratio is too low," or "the debt to equity ratio is too high," or "there is inadequate capitalization," or "the history of good profits is not long enough." In that case, have the guarantee reduced each year as you continue to improve your ratios until such time as the guarantee is eliminated, i.e., when you have achieved the goals you and the lender have agreed upon. Make certain to put this agreement in writing as bank officers come and go, and oral understandings may be forgotten.

In many cases, our clients have *blindly* signed guarantees because they assume it is expected of them. I recall one friend of mine who had signed guarantees with his bank for the past fifteen years. He had an amazingly well run company. Just to prove my point, we visited the bank together and asked for the personal guarantee to be removed. The bank said *yes*. My friend was astounded. "I didn't realize it was that easy," he said. I quizzed him, "Had you ever asked the bank before? They are not going to volunteer that you end your guarantee." He had never asked.

Remember, the guarantee always will be included in the loan package. If you are truly **Healthy**, you may not have to sign it as written. Executives of **Healthy** companies know this.

ONGOING HEALTH CHECKS

Companies, like people, need to check out their **health** annually. We submit ourselves to all sorts of medical tests because we know that early detection is the best form of prevention. This is also true of a living, breathing organization. As previously mentioned, Kibel Green Issa Inc. developed a comprehensive 49-page questionnaire to assist our consultants in establishing a company's position on the **Corporate Clock**. Other organizations have their own methods. However it is done, it is important to look at organization structure, employee talent, systems and technical support, product/service quality, financial and operating information, etc. Each of these must be evaluated objectively. It is hard for fellow executives to be critical of each other. It is impossible to know if your infrastructure is weak in relation to that of your competition. This takes knowledge of the world beyond your company. Not keeping up with the outside world would be like seeing a doctor who is not current about the latest research and, as a result, fails to cure you of a serious problem when, all the while, that cure was known to experts in the field. Operating expenses often differ by orders of magnitude between the best and worst run companies in the same industry. The difference is often in the proper use of the latest technology.

When the **health** check indicates there is a problem, the **Healthy** company immediately goes into action and makes the necessary corrections. Its officers understand that all **Healthy** organizations drift into the **Crossroads** zone from time to time. The secret is to catch problems early — and correct them. When business is going well, management feels that this effort is a waste of time. When business is in trouble, it is too late to perform such an analysis. When an organization is **Healthy**, it has the financial strength to correct its problems. That is why top executives of **Healthy-Healthy** companies perform their **health** checks as part of the cost of doing business. Most **health** checks produce direct savings far in excess of the cost. They are good investments in their own right.

Many companies with strong financials think they are **Healthy**. When their business is in the expansion phase of the economic cycle and there is little competition, they will have good financials. This does not mean, however, that they are well run. The cycle, at some point, will turn downward. Then the test of real **health** will come. If a company possesses the other elements of good **health** discussed in this chapter, it will not only survive but will use the downward cycle to acquire weak competitors and strengthen its market position. It will be able to withstand the economic down turn because its information system will alert the company to problems well in advance. Strategic and Contingency Planning will be in place, ready for implementation. The organization will be fine tuned in response to the marketplace, customers, and vendors. Lenders will work with the company because, long ago, the leadership cultivated excellent relationships. The business knows how to take advantage of the capital markets, and has a handle on the major problem areas. The Balance Sheet is strong and well managed. There is excellent communication between the leadership and all personnel, and none of the net worth has been put at risk. The company is **HEALTHY**!

SUMMARY

All companies that remain in this first quadrant will have a long life. They are well organized. There is access to the top executive or owner. They plan, not only for good times, but for bad times as well. Compensation is fair. Executives are given the authority they need to get their jobs done. The informal structure matches the formal organization, and all share the corporate vision. The company's existing financials are strong, both in an absolute sense and in relation to the rest of the industry. Information is timely and useful so that action can be taken and results measured. Programs in sales and marketing are integrated. Important policies and procedures are documented. The organization is sensitive to the importance of maintaining good relationships with employees, vendors, customers, shareholders, lenders, and regulatory agencies. The top executive is *plugged in* to the top vendors, customers, key executives, and lenders. He or she can pick up the phone and reach the decision-maker in any one of these organizations. Executive talent is high; turnover is low, and customers pay promptly. The company is sensitive to the environment, to sexual harassment, and to wrongful termination issues, and has been proactive in preventing or minimizing problems in these areas.

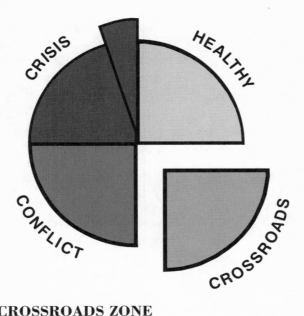

THE CROSSROADS ZONE

Dark clouds begin to appear on the horizon. A company in this quadrant is uncomfortable and senses that time is beginning to accelerate. The CEO feels like the manufacturer of gas lamps who reads about a fellow named Thomas Edison in the newspaper, or like the buggy maker who gets a sinking feeling when he hears about Henry Ford's new vehicle. All **Healthy** companies drift into the **Crossroads** zone at one time or another. **Healthy** companies become aware of problems quickly and make the necessary corrections. Companies destined for greater problems, however, put on their rose colored glasses and assume that the *good old days* are just around the corner. Danger signs are everywhere, but relatively few companies see them and take action.

The danger in this phase is that everything still seems to be all right. Profit and Loss and Balance Sheet Statements show a declining pattern, but the absolute numbers are acceptable. Cash Flow is adequate, but deteriorating. There are periodic breakdowns in the system, but they generally work satisfactorily. Management reports are usually late and filled with inaccuracies, but they were probably late even when business was good. Sometimes there is a flurry of Strategic Planning and some Contingency Planning, but this is clearly not an important element in the corporate culture. In general, there is a big difference between the talent at the upper levels and the rest of the organization. The informal organization functions as a separate entity, bearing little relationship to the organization charts that were drawn up but never used. Compensation is tied to political pull, seniority, and type of skill, rather than performance. Customers and· vendors have been assigned to lower level staff in the organization. Therefore, top management has little feel for the real-world marketplace. Corporate **health** is a poorly understood concept and is rarely monitored.

Ties to sources of capital and debt are weak. Communication is faulty. Dark clouds are appearing on the horizon for all to see, but the level of optimism still runs high in the souls of most executives. Management believes the clouds will blow away if they wait and conduct business as usual. The secondary level executives, however, who are more security minded, see the handwriting on the wall. They may even have tried, with little success, to communicate the impending doom they see before them to the CEO, but they are caught between the proverbial *rock and a hard place*. If they push too hard on the chief executive, they could get fired, but if they do nothing, they will be out of a company. Short-term thinking generally prevails, and the CEO is allowed to live in his or her *fairy tale world*. But the company's shortcomings will not heal themselves. Unattended, they will become the cancer everyone hopes to avoid.

Unfortunately, the golden opportunity to correct the company's problems will be lost if the **Crossroads** phase is not recognized now. Companies in this phase are **healthy** enough to have the resources needed for addressing the potential problems. Too many executives are used to putting out fires and have less skill in anticipating potential crises. The cigarette industry is a good example. It has wisely concluded that the long-term prognosis for smoking in the United States is poor. Organizations such as the American Cancer Society have begun a campaign to make smoking socially unacceptable. These companies, while benefiting from their cigarette businesses, have also begun to acquire businesses outside of their industry. In time, these outside interests may save their companies. This does not mean that they are not fighting to keep things alive for as long as possible, but they have a Strategic Plan to more than survive when their *core* business declines. Morton Salt has experimented with the air bag. E-Systems is adapting the digital image storage and retrieval systems it developed for radiography, using what it has learned about tanks, submarines, and spy satellites, to search for tumors in mammograms. These companies realize that they need to be protected from change by preparing for it.

Companies that break out of the **Crossroads** quadrant utilize one or more of the following strategies:

- They expand existing products and services to new markets that will not be negatively affected by the economy.

- They use their resources to create new products and services for existing markets.

- They take the greater risk of providing new products and services for new markets.

E-Systems is an example of the first strategy, and Morton Salt is an example of the third. An example of the second strategy could be Clayton Homes, which not only *manufactures* homes, but also *retails, finances,* and *manages* communities of manufactured homes. Mercedes Benz has added a passenger van and a sport utility vehicle to its powerful sedan line. The oil companies' transition of selling fast food at service stations and the Big Six accounting firms' aggressive entry into the consulting field are recent examples of this strategy.

Unfortunately, for most companies, it's *business as usual.* They will watch their businesses decline, thinking that downsizing and praying are their only options. But, evidently, the old adage is true: "God helps those who help themselves."

The problems that have appeared are in their early stages. They can be addressed at minimal cost because there are more than adequate resources and plenty of time to make the necessary corrections.

The characteristics of the **Crossroads** quadrant have the same elements as those of the **Healthy** zone, but in many areas, the company has started to slide downhill.

- The Balance Sheet is growing weaker but it is still acceptable.

- Profits and margins are down, but the company is still making money.

- Cash flow is tighter. Bills are being paid, albeit a bit slower.

- Management reports are usually late and inaccurate, but this is nothing new. The information system is not useful as a tool for addressing financial and operational problems.

- The difference between the level of talent at the top and the levels below are now obvious. Those at the lower levels are not accustomed to being, nor were they hired to be, innovative leaders.

- The informal structure has divided into camps and it

bears no relationship to the formal organization structure.

- There is no real compensation system.   People are advanced based on pull or seniority rather than merit.

- Top management is not connected to its secured lenders.

- Top management is not closely connected to its customer base or to its key vendors.

- Communication between key executives is rapidly falling apart.

- There is no *cry for action,* no sense of urgency. Complacency prevents timely action.

THE BALANCE SHEET IS ACCEPTABLE, BUT WEAKER

Many executives focus their attention on the Profit and Loss Statement, often ignoring the important information being provided by the Balance Sheet. This is easy to do because the outside world tends to focus on revenue and earnings per share without paying close attention to the leveraging of the business. In a general way, we all realize, that once a business runs out of cash, *the ball game is over.* The Balance Sheet provides the information needed to measure that risk.   Fixed assets, inventory, and accounts receivable ultimately must be converted into cash. If a business has borrowed heavily against these assets, it will benefit in an expanding economic environment but will decline more rapidly when the economy contracts. A company having a net worth of $5 million with $100 million in assets and $95 million in liabilities can ill afford a 5% reduction in the value of its assets. A company with a net worth of $5 million with $20 million in assets and

$15 million in liabilities can absorb a 5% reduction in the value of its assets. In fact, assets would have to decline by 25% before the net worth would be lost. The facts are evident in the Balance Sheet.

There are certain key ratios that should be examined. The first is the current ratio, which measures working capital and is a good index for cash flow. It is calculated by dividing current assets by current liabilities. In general, the larger the ratio, the lower the leverage and the lower the risk. Preferably this ratio should be 1.5 to 1.0 or more. Current assets should be at least 1.5 times current liabilities to insure that there is sufficient liquidity to meet the ongoing operating needs of the business. In certain industries, this is not possible. The movement of current assets toward cash must flow at a faster pace than the cash needed to meet the needs of the banks, vendors and ongoing asset requirements.

Second in importance is the debt to equity ratio. It really should be calculated by dividing total liabilities by tangible net worth. Other ratios, such as inventory turnover, also should be monitored.

As a company moves into the **Crossroads** quadrant, these key ratios begin to slip. Cash flow shortages are addressed by borrowing more money and paying back vendors at a slower pace. Unfortunately, this approach can only lead to disaster. A company cannot borrow its way to good **health** or maximize its margins and sources of material with unhappy vendors. It is only a question of time before vendors put the business on C.O.D. and limit purchasing power.

If a business is beginning to deteriorate, this is the time to reduce its size in an orderly manner so the revised entity can produce sufficient cash flow to meet the ongoing needs of the business. When the economy strengthens, expansion can be rejuvenated, albeit at a slower pace. Alternatively, a company could bring in equity to meet its cash flow needs and continue to grow. This could be accomplished through a private placement, a public offering, or special programs (such as the creation of an ESOP).

Usually, however, the Balance Sheet continues to deteriorate in the **Crossroads** phase, and management takes no action.

PROFITS ARE DOWN — BUT THE BUSINESS IS STILL PROFITABLE

The **Crossroads** phase can be a somewhat lethargic time. Profits and margins are down, but survival does not appear to be an issue. If the company can *only hold on,* the *good old days* will return, and once again it will enjoy the level of profits it knew in prior years. Management tries to avoid taking a hard look at the facts. The pattern of reduced margins indicates that, unless they take some action (or a miracle occurs), they will begin losing money some time in the near future. *Murphy's Law* threatens that the downward pattern is likely to continue, and that a miracle is unlikely. There is still time to make the necessary corrections. Should they get out of certain product or service lines? Can they take steps in purchasing to improve margins on raw materials? Can changes be made in operations to reduce costs, including reduction in labor and overhead? Should some operations that have been kept in house be outsourced? Should part of the business be sold? Can space requirements be reduced? Are the executive group and the support system too large for current business needs? Should everyone be taking reduced or deferred compensation to demonstrate that austerity is required?

In this phase, it takes so little to make an enormous difference. A company doing $50 million in sales and making a minimal pre-tax profit of $1 million has incurred $49 million in expenses. As little as a 5% reduction in expenses would add $2.45 million to profits, raising it to a respectable $3.45 million, even if sales remain flat! In my experience, I've found it possible to reduce costs by at least ten percent if the problem is approached from the top down. That would add

$4.9 million to the pre-tax profits.

Unfortunately, nothing is done to stabilize the company, and it moves out of the **Crossroads** phase toward **Conflict** and into **Crisis**.

THE MANAGEMENT INFORMATION SYSTEM IS NOT USEFUL FOR ADDRESSING FINANCIAL AND OPERATIONAL PROBLEMS

One of the early signs of deterioration of a business is the inability of management to get good information. When the company was making money, monthly financial reports showing overall Profit and Loss and Balance Sheet data were adequate. Typically, these reports were accounting oriented. They often included cost allocations, which made it impossible to connect costs with individual executive responsibility. Departmental and/or product performance records usually were not available because, when people are making money, *nobody cares.*

Suddenly, management *discovers* that profit margins are down and that the Balance Sheet is deteriorating. They desperately need information that can indicate what action(s) must be taken, and they need reports that reflect the effects of the action(s). Should they drop certain products? It's hard to tell if you don't know profitability by product. Should you reduce certain costs? If so, in which department? More importantly, who will be responsible for the cost reduction? If the information system doesn't separate fixed from variable costs and controllable from non-controllable expenses, it is difficult to know how to address the problem. A department or product line may look bad because it absorbs a large, unreasonable portion of certain fixed costs. If that department or product were to be eliminated, these costs would have to be allocated elsewhere. They would not, however, go away! In the final analysis, if the reports do not tie costs to responsibilities, it is difficult to manage the cost reduction program.

Inaccuracies are another problem that is seldom addressed when business is good. At the end of the year, outside accountants come in and correct the inventories, reserves, receivables and payable balances. If these end-of-the-year adjustments are significant, it means that the information reported over the past eleven months has been inaccurate. A third problem is late reporting. If the reports are not received promptly, they become nothing more than a historical record and lose their usefulness as an action tool.

At the **Crossroads** level, there is plenty of time to redesign the management information system to make it responsive to the needs of the business. Unfortunately, management tries, instead, to give the old system a kick, hoping it will work as it did in the *good old days*. The problem is that it never worked in the *good old days* either — but *nobody cared*.

TALENT AT THE TOP IS DIFFERENT FROM THAT AT THE LEVELS BELOW

Second and third level executives usually can identify problems in the early stages. They know there are employee problems, inefficiencies, and difficulty in selling the product or service. They are *out there* every day fighting the battle. In a **healthy** organization, any early signs of weakness are immediately communicated *upstairs*. No time is wasted, and action is taken. If the sales department is beginning to experience resistance, steps are taken to find out why. Is the product or service becoming obsolete? Do you have new competition? Is there a serious quality problem? Are you not providing something important that the competition is supplying? Are there rumors about the company's financial stability? If caught early, these problems can be addressed properly. If caught late, there could be a disaster.

Many companies that drift into the **Crossroads** quadrant

have a long history of dictatorial leadership by top management. Good lieutenants receive instructions and dutifully carry them out. Their job is to execute commands and not ask questions. Therefore, when they sense problems in their area of expertise, they do not see it as their job to report this information to top management. After all, top management never was interested in their ideas in the past. In fact, the second level people who tried to be too innovative have already been culled out of the organization. It can be dangerous to tell top management that they have a problem. They want to hear that "everything is okay."

As the problems increase, it takes more executive horsepower to right the ship. When second and third level talent is nonexistent, the task at the top becomes monumental. The problems have not yet become acute, so top management lulls themselves into believing that all will soon be well if they can just hold on and conduct business as usual.

It is at this juncture that management should take steps to change their corporate culture. They should meet with key second and third level management personnel to let them know that their input is valued and that they are part of the team. Those middle management people who cannot rise to the occasion because of their mental set or because of their capability limitations should either be transferred or replaced. This is an opportunity to upgrade the lower levels.

If the company were to move into the **Conflict** or **Crisis** phase without strong second and third level management, it probably would be doomed to failure. It takes a team to bring a company back into the **Healthy** quadrant. The further along the company is on the **Clock**, the stronger the team must be to get the job done.

The key obstacle is that top management often does not recognize the importance of having innovative talent at the mid-executive levels. Talented, innovative people are harder to manage. They have ideas of their own. They won't follow blindly and, at times, can be difficult to manage. Top executives of **healthy** companies put up with this because they know it is important to long-term **health**.

THERE IS SIGNIFICANT VARIANCE BETWEEN THE FORMAL AND INFORMAL ORGANIZATION STRUCTURE

Often, when I visit a company in the early stages of decline, the top executive will proudly show me an organization chart clearly identifying each position and the reporting relationships throughout the organization. In many cases, these charts are further supported by detailed job descriptions that summarize each job, its responsibilities, authority and reporting relationships. It's quite impressive to see. I generally ask, politely, if I can construct a *bottom-up* organization chart. "It's real simple," I explain to them. "I just start at the bottom of the organization and ask each person who they report to, and what they and their boss do each day." In **healthy** organizations, there is usually a great deal of congruency between the formal chart and the informal reality of the organization. We find, however, when a company moves into the **Crossroads** quadrant, this congruency breaks down.

At one major financial institution in Los Angeles, I showed the Chairman of the Board and CEO that there was an Executive Vice President to whom no one reported. "That's impossible!", he uttered. "How could that happen?" We looked for the answer to that question and discovered that this Executive Vice President had made himself inconspicuous and obsolete five years ago. He did not keep up with the dramatic changes taking place in the industry. When his subordinates went to him with questions, he was of no help. Gradually, they began to go to the Vice President in charge of loans because he had the answers. Over time, they stopped asking the Executive Vice President any questions at all, and began reporting to the Vice President of Loans. When asked the question, "Who do you report to?" in our bottoms-up analysis, they naturally answered, "the Vice President of Loans." In the informal structure, he had, in effect, become the Executive Vice President. Everyone knew about this change except the Chairman of the Board and CEO who clung to his outdated organization charts and couldn't understand why things weren't getting done. Why didn't he know? In this case, it was out of kindness. The Executive Vice President was a nice man. He would come to the office each day, keep his door closed and hope he would not be discovered. Give this man credit. He kept the charade going for five years! I am convinced that, at some point, the truth would have come out because the Vice President of Loans would want to be recognized. We recommended that the Vice President of Loans be formally promoted to Executive Vice President since it had already happened five years ago.

The lesson is clear. Do not be blinded by charts and curves. Make certain you know what really is going on. It is the informal structure that counts; the rest is useless paperwork. In fact, I am beginning to question the value of too many charts. They tend to stagnate the organization and prevent executives from crossing over the lines when that is clearly the best way to get the job done.

To bring your company back into the **Healthy** quadrant, everyone must be working together. Middle management, as well as the rank and file, must feel that the top executives know what is going on in the organization and that everyone has a shared vision to solve the problem.

COMPENSATION IS NOT BASED ON MERIT

When a business is thriving, there is often a tendency for the top executives to take full credit for its magnificent performance. I might add, however, that when the business declines, the very same executives will blame the government, unfair competition, and the economy before they will take personal responsibility. During the **Healthy** period, when egos are a bit inflated, compensation tends to be random. If top management likes an executive, they may be more generous with him or her. Over time, compensation tends to get out of control. Mediocre talent with good marks in personality and aggressiveness are earning more than very talented people who are less politically astute. The problem is that, at the lower levels, everyone knows who is really performing and who is pulling his/her own weight. Employees see the individuals in action every day. They cannot be fooled.

When a company drifts into **Crossroads**, it is generally safe to say that the internal financial information system, as previously described, is weak. Top management, therefore, is never in a good position to measure the real performance of a given manager. *Gut feel* is the key to getting ahead and being rewarded. Unfortunately, as the organization begins to weaken, the more talented people get more frustrated with the *dead wood* that have been unfairly rewarded. Since they are the *best and the brightest* in the organization, they are also the most marketable. They may depart from the company, leaving management with the *dead wood* to bring the business back into the **Healthy** zone. Or they may decide to stay but work at a much slower pace. The logic is, "If I am being unfairly compensated, I may as well lower my commitment to the organization so that it matches my pay." The problem could be compounded if they decide to stay and bad mouth top management. That could create a rift in the organization that might help to move it rapidly in the wrong direction — toward the **Crisis** quadrant.

Our studies have shown that the fairness of compensation within an organization is more important than the fairness of compensation as it relates to the marketplace. We have also learned that compensation never can be kept secret. Confidential payrolls do not work. People are too curious and, one way or another, will figure out who gets what.

Therefore, salaries must be fair. They must be based on objective performance and must agree with middle management's as well as the rank and file's perception of who is performing. This requires both a reasonable compensation system and an information system that enables the company to measure performance.

If the business is going to return to the **Healthy** quadrant, it will need the help of those people who make the greatest contribution. If they feel they have been fairly rewarded in the past, they generally will be sufficiently loyal to stay and help right the ship.

If the business is in the **Crossroads** quadrant, one must take a hard look at the compensation system. There is more than enough time to correct the situation. However, if that time is wasted, the talent will begin to leave, and the problems of bringing the business back to good **health** will be more difficult to accomplish.

TOP MANAGEMENT IS NOT CONNECTED TO THE SECURED LENDERS

When a business is doing well and one can select the best deal from many different financial institutions, there is little motivation to develop a close working relationship with the lender(s). Responsibility for this relationship is generally passed on to the Chief Financial Officer who then interacts with the bank's account officer. As long as the company stays in the **Healthy** zone, the relationship appears to work. Everyone is happy. The bank is lending money to a **Healthy** borrower who always pays its bills on time. *Yes, sir! They're one big, happy family!* Should they get into trouble, however, the bank's account manager will inform them that he has no real authority, but will do his best to present their case to his superiors on the loan committee. If things get really bad, this account manager will disappear and the account will be transferred to the Workout Department (which goes by different names in each financial institution). For the first time, the top executive will meet the decision-maker at the financial institution. He/she will be looking for some relief, extension of the line, restructuring of the debt, deferral of principal payments, etc.

The bank executive will see this person as a statistic he has read about in some reports. The account executive may have mentioned the firm in passing. It will be easy to turn down this individual. It is always easier to say *no* than *yes*. After all, the loan officer has no personal knowledge of the individual or the firm. The bank didn't create the problem, and they don't want to go through a long period of uncertainty. The company's choices are to locate another bank, accept the existing lender's ominous terms, sell, or liquidate.

Now let me rewrite this script. Mr. D, owner of ABC Company, is doing very well. Sales and profits are up and he has a strong Balance Sheet. He is currently considered a genius in his industry (but knows this reputation won't last forever). Mr. D also recognizes that good times are not set in concrete. He finds out who in the lender organization makes the decisions related to his account. It is Mr. E. Mr. D finds out if Mr. E is married, how many children he has, his hobbies and interests, his background and business orientation. Mr. D then sets up an appointment to meet Mr. E. They share their common background. Both of them were brought up in the streets of New York. They discover they have children going to the same school, and they both enjoy a good game of tennis. Mr. E is a staunch conservative and Mr. D is quite liberal. Mr. D decides he will stay away from the subject of politics. Mr. D invites Mr. E for tennis at his club. They play tennis with each other on some reasonable basis. They come to know each other on a personal level. In the meantime, the Chief Financial Officer is still meeting with the account executive. Now, as the ABC company moves into the **Crossroads** quadrant, Mr. D bypasses the account executive and calls Mr. E directly. He explains that he could use some short-term relief from the bank and they work something out.

I have often seen two companies with similar problems in similar businesses with equal opportunities for survival. Yet, it is the one who has an excellent relationship with its financial source that survives.

I hope I have made my point. The economy goes up and down. It has been doing this since our country began. The secret of long-term survival lies in the way top management handles the down cycles. However, it is only during the up cycles that these important relationships can be developed.

TOP MANAGEMENT IS NOT CLOSELY CONNECTED TO ITS KEY CUSTOMERS AND VENDORS

The issue here is similar to the failure to connect at the highest level with the secured lender. When a business is **healthy**, the top executive will often delegate the responsibility of connecting with key customers to the Vice President of Sales and/or Marketing. After all, that's his/her job. In a similar manner, the responsibility for connecting with the key vendors would be delegated to the Vice President of Manufacturing and/or Purchasing because that's his/her job! Doing it this way seems to make sense, but it is a bad idea.

I was recently dealing with two companies that were in trouble. Both owned a chain of retail stores. Both provided hardware and appliances for the home. They had similar financial statements and both had been in business for a long time. One company spent a lot of time with its key vendors. The CEO knew the decision-makers in the vendor organization on a first name basis. They played golf and tennis together, and knew each other's families. We spent a few days meeting with these vendors, explaining that we had some short-term cash flow problems and needed them to help by dramatically extending terms over the next six months. All of the key vendors accommodated. Enough time was bought to bring the company back into the **Healthy** quadrant. The second company ignored its vendors who were unwilling to extend any credit. Instead, we had to negotiate with the secured lender who also had limited contact at the upper levels with our client. For the second company, the restructuring was costly. The first company, in effect, received an extension of credit at zero percent interest. The second paid higher interest rates to the secured lender and, in addition, had to provide additional collateral and guarantees. The difference between the two companies was simply their respective relationships with their vendors.

The same is true with customer relations. Customers can help you out at times. They can even accelerate your receivables. Moreover, they are an excellent source of information about your competition, your reputation, and the needs of the marketplace. These relationships, however, must be cultivated during the good times. That's why it is so important for top management to keep its *hands on the steering wheel* when everything is going well and to connect with its peers in both vendor and customer organizations.

When I speak to the Young Presidents' Organization, World Presidents' Organization, and Chief Executives' Organization and The Executive Committee groups across the country, I always stress that 30% of executives' time should be spent cultivating relationships with their *sources* of capital, products and services as well as with the *recipients* of their products and services. I further suggest that they open up their date books and begin the process of scheduling meetings with these key individuals. Relationships are extremely important in getting the support required during the **Crossroads** phase when, in most cases, all you need is time.

COMMUNICATION IS WEAK BETWEEN KEY EXECUTIVES

In **healthy** companies that begin to drift into the **Crossroads** quadrant, I find that business has been conducted from the top down. Loyal lieutenants carry out orders issued by top management. The concept of true give and take is not generally part of the corporate culture. Sometimes, for example, when I look at the financial information, I find ample evidence that business has declined. I invariably ask the Chief Financial Officer if this decline has been discussed with top management. The answer I usually get is *"no!"* Their response is often that "top management only wants to hear good news. They get angry when told there are serious problems, so we bring them good news and otherwise remain silent." Does this sound familiar? How many times has a Chief Financial Officer been told that the reports were *all screwed up* because management didn't like what they were reading? An even greater problem is the inability of the top executive to read the financials properly, particularly the Balance Sheet. Was the company aware of the deterioration in Cash Flow, the slowing of Receivables, the stretching of Payables, the increase in Capital Expenditures over Budget, or the slowing down of Inventory Turnover? If the Chief Financial Officer is reluctant to bring these problems to the attention of top management, the trouble spot(s) could become a cancer that destroys the organization.

Good communication is more than a pep talk. It involves knowing your people as well as understanding their personal and business problems. It is active listening, not issuing instructions from on high. It is accepting downside information without *shooting the messenger.* It is sharing your vision with your team and modifying that vision as you listen until everyone understands and agrees. Without the *buy in,* there is no loyalty. Without loyalty, the leaders will jump ship when you need them most.

An *open door policy* must be in place when problems arise. Anyone, at any level, should have access to the top. It is amazing how much the rank and file know. Employees often can alert you to problems long before they become serious. This will only happen if they have real access to you, and if you keep the information confidential at all times. These people are vulnerable and need your protection. They also tend to be fiercely loyal.

Communication is more than having meetings. Are your meetings merely mechanical, *show and tell* sessions? Is the goal to impress top management and avoid discussing any issues that are either controversial or reflect badly on the competence of the officers? When a company drifts into **Crossroads**, the energy of its key people must be highly focused. If they communicate honestly and share a common vision, their energy can be focused directly on the singular task of moving the company back into the **Healthy** quadrant.

THERE IS NO CRY FOR ACTION

The reason why so many companies in the **Crossroads** phase drift into the **Conflict** quadrant is *complacency*. It is easy to tell yourself that "This, too, shall pass." What is necessary is a sense of urgency, and that must begin at the top. It takes a secure and competent executive to admit that (1) deterioration is taking place; and (2) something must be done about it. This sense of urgency starts at the top and ultimately must be felt in all parts of the organization. It generally requires a symbolic sense of sacrifice. Management may have to admit that it has made some mistakes. Once acknowledged, they must be corrected. In some cases, key executives have taken pay cuts or salary deferrals until the company is brought back into the **Healthy** quadrant. The sacrifice lets everyone know that the problem is urgent. Often, other executives will offer to make similar sacrifices.

If, in the **Crossroads** phase, the problems are recognized and addressed, it is an easy matter to return the business to good **health**.

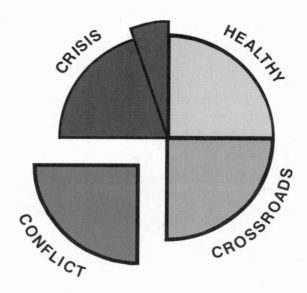

THE CONFLICT ZONE

When a company moves into the **Conflict** phase, it is clear that it is in trouble. There is evidence of problems all around. They must be dealt with now, with the organization in a much more deteriorated condition. What are these problems?

• The company begins to lose money.

• The company is in violation of its loan agreements.

• Cash flow is marginal.

• Systems are actually breaking down.

- There is an exodus of the *best and the brightest.*

- Planning is non-existent.

- The banks are on the verge of calling in the loan.

THE COMPANY IS AT A BREAKEVEN POINT OR INCURRING SOME LOSS

It is clear now that business is declining. Sales and margins are down. The company is no longer profitable, and the slide looks like it might continue. The top executives are calling emergency meetings and asking how this could have happened. They inevitably blame the problem on someone or something outside of their control. The culprit could be the economy, competition, or the government. Action, however, must be taken. Usually, some forms of across the board reductions are implemented that have not been well thought out. The key executive team will remain, of course, but lower level personnel will be let go. The company may strip itself unwittingly of key operating people needed to get its product out the door while retaining high paid executives and their entourages until it is too late. The executives are not going to recommend their own demise, although we have discovered that the big savings, the breakthrough savings, come from reducing the size and consolidating the management team. This involves the elimination and combining of departments.

Meanwhile, down in the rank and file, there exists additional knowledge about how to improve the profitability of the business. In most situations, they never will be asked. Those executives responsible for getting the company into a loss position will now be charged with the task of turning the business back to profitability. Before that happens, they have to protect their own position, which often means protecting each other. To make certain that the finger is not pointed at them, they must remain politically astute. In this kind of environment, is it any wonder that nothing serious gets done and the company continues to drift into **Crisis**? This is one time when unbiased, experienced, outside advice is needed. Who else will recommend reorganization of the business? Who else will recommend that certain empires be merged, outsourced or eliminated? Who else can point out where overstaffing truly exists, and avoid the across the board approach that only punishes the efficient departments?

The willingness of top management to take responsibility for the problem and bring in the talent and experience necessary to move the business back toward the **Healthy** quadrant is essential. Hard decisions must be made — soon. Time is accelerating. Procrastination at this juncture can be extremely dangerous.

THE COMPANY IS IN TECHNICAL VIOLATION OF ITS LOAN AGREEMENT WITH ITS SECURED LENDER

This is the first signal to the outside world that the company is in trouble. Typically, the lender has established key ratios, which often include: debt to equity, current assets to current liabilities, and formulas that relate receivables and inventories to the level of borrowing.

When any of these key indices are violated, the company is said to be in technical violation of its loan agreement, even though principal and interest payments are still being made on time. The bank generally will not call in the loan for that reason, but will put the company under greater scrutiny. Higher-level executives may follow the account and even want to meet with the top management of the company. It is important that, during this period, the company does not play with "float" and run the risk of an overdraft position. If this occurs, it sends up *red flags* throughout the lending institution.

Some top executives believe that as long as they are making their loan payments on time, the bank will not bother them. This is not true. Banks have learned that the earlier they address a problem company, the lower their risk of loss. In fact, in today's environment, the lenders seem to be less interested in going through a workout. They either want the problems solved quickly or the company to find a new lender. If they suspect that the loan is under-collateralized, they may move it into the Workout Department even though payments are current. The lender may be interested in the trade accounts payable. Are these creditors being severely stretched in order to stay current with the bank? If so, it is only a matter of time before there will be a monetary default. The proper response of top management should be proactive. They should develop a Plan showing that they recognize the problems and are prepared to take specific actions to correct them. They even may have to ask the lender for some temporary relief. If the lender sees the Plan as reasonable and has had confidence in management in the past, there is probably some room for negotiation. The Plan should include milestones so the lender can objectively measure the progress of the business in solving its problems.

Unfortunately, in most cases, nothing happens. Communication between the lender and the borrower breaks down. Negative information is delayed and withheld. Mistrust begins to fill the air, and the first time the company has a monetary default, the bank comes crashing down on it. This is a sad situation because all of these problems could have been avoided.

CASH FLOW IS MARGINAL

Cash is tight now. It is no longer possible to pay all the bills on time. Vendors are calling and asking to be paid. The company is employing all the usual stall tactics: forgetting to sign a check, making partial rather than full payments, saying "the check is in the mail" and then forgetting to mail it, not answering phone calls, etc. Many times, checks are printed and held until there is *daylight* in the cash flow, or a critical vendor threatens to cut off the company's supply of product.

Cash flow has become a company-wide problem. It is necessary to meet at least once a week to decide how much money is available and who the lucky recipients of the cash will be. In many cases, the money will go to favorite customers and to those who yell and threaten the loudest. Cooperative, non-critical vendors are dragged the most, particularly the professionals who have no leverage once they have performed their service. There is usually a great effort to keep the bank(s) current as long as possible. The hope is that they will be the last ones to know. When they do find out, it will be a surprise. Banks don't like surprises. They assume that you were either withholding information from them or were so far out of control that you didn't know you were in trouble. Either way, management has a credibility problem, and the lender will be wary of dealing with the company in the future.

Often, cash planning is weak because Balance Sheet reporting, in general, is weak. It becomes necessary to install a cash planning system at this time. The executives are beginning to understand that the management of assets and liabilities has become more important than the management of the Profit and Loss Statement. Surviving in the short run involves converting receivables and inventory to cash as quickly as possible while stretching vendor payables to their limits. This game can only be played for so long. If the company is not restored to profitability, time must be bought in some other way. This can occur through the injection of capital into the business but more often involves restructuring the debt with the existing secured lender.

Therefore, the last supplier the company should alienate is the supplier of money. Lenders should be informed promptly when problems surface. They should receive the Cash Flow reports and find comfort in knowing that the company is taking corrective action. If the business needs relief in the near future, this should be discussed in time for the bank to go through its normal decision-making process. If the lender participates in the solutions, the credibility problem will be avoided.

I try to explain to my clients (many of whom have been *Profit and Loss* oriented for all of their business careers) that **when you run out of cash, the ball game is over**. If you can't pay your bills, you run the risk of being put into an involuntary bankruptcy filing by your creditors. Even if this does not happen, the company reaches a point where a downward spiral is created. Your creditors either stop shipping critical raw materials, or they put you on C.O.D., which further exacerbates your cash flow problem. If you can't get the necessary raw materials, you can't make the finished product, and sales come crashing down faster than the reduction in demand. In time, the company cannot operate.

In the **Conflict** phase, the problem is apparent. There is still time to take corrective action, but that time is accelerating dramatically as the company moves toward a possible **crisis**.

THE ACCOUNTING AND INFORMATION SYSTEM IS BREAKING DOWN

In the **Conflict** stage, it is abundantly clear that the accounting and information system is breaking down. Reports are very late. I have worked with some companies in which the financials were six months late. It seems as if the Accounting Department becomes overwhelmed. Typically, current information is not available. A report delivered one month late is better than nothing in that kind of environment, but it is still useless for making any proactive decisions. The last thing an executive in the **Conflict** period needs is an inaccurate historical report that reflects how the business is deteriorating. At this stage, it is usually an accepted fact that the reports are not accurate. If management is unhappy with what the report says, they can blame the Accounting Department. But this only masks the reality that the company is sliding rapidly toward the **Crisis** quadrant. The inaccuracies, of course, are not only the fault of the Accounting Department. Possibly in an attempt to make everything look as good as possible, the Sales Department may be sending poor revenue information to Accounting. The information coming out of Operations also may be distorted.

I was once called in by a major public company because they had a significant shortfall from the earnings they had promised Wall Street. The culprit was one wholly-owned subsidiary. It had a major inventory adjustment large enough to raise doubt in the value of the eleven months' worth of reports it had provided. I immediately sensed that the real problems had to be in Operations. As it turned out, the company had an incentive system in which workers' pay was based on their output. It was common knowledge that output was exaggerated at each stage of production. The workers knew that the company did not have the information system necessary to control the accuracy of the output reports. The only reason prior years did not result in similar adjustments was that the Controller knew the system didn't work. He refused to blow the whistle on anyone. Instead, he estimated monthly adjustments to both the Profit and Loss Statement and the Balance Sheet to account for the cheating. Unfortunately, that Controller left the company at the beginning of the year. The subsidiary, therefore, reported outstanding interim earnings, which the parent company accepted until the audit was conducted at the end of the year. The subsidiary was losing money, but the fact wasn't made *public* until 90 days after the end of the fiscal year.

In another company, the lower levels of management (whom no one speaks to) knew for many years that the information system was a disaster. They developed their own back pocket methods for keeping track of what was really going on. This was the most successful manufacturing facility of a public company in the food processing business. It was the most profitable of the fifteen plants run by the company. Most of the other Plant Managers were of the new *best and the brightest* breed with MBAs from some of the top schools in the country. Joe, however, clearly did not have a college education. He recognized that the new production and inventory control system designed by their high tech personnel was useless. While the MBAs relied on the system for many years, Joe placed the reports neatly in a file and never looked at them. He had his own *black book,* which he used to record what was really going on. When I looked at his file of inventory reports, they were so neat I could tell they hadn't been looked at. After much probing, Joe finally showed me his back pocket report and explained why the production and inventory management system was *baloney.* (These were not his exact words but you get my drift.) I suggested to top management that we scrap the existing system and use Joe's back pocket system as the basis for the new production and inventory control system. I also suggested that experienced operational people be involved in the creation of their new system — a novel idea which management accepted.

It is hard enough to solve the problems in business even if you receive all the facts in a timely manner. Management is usually forced to *shoot from the hip* when the facts are not there. Often, by *shooting from the hip,* you wind up shooting yourself in the foot.

KEY PERSONNEL ARE BEGINNING TO FLEE

At this stage, it is obvious that key personnel are looking for work elsewhere. They see that the ship is sinking and want to be long gone before they are associated with a failing business.

The most talented and intelligent people already have figured out that the company is in trouble. They are also aware that management is not capable of taking the right steps. They have not developed any great sense of loyalty for all the reasons mentioned earlier. Worst of all, they are the *most marketable* of the staff. They probably sent out resumes during the latter part of the **Crossroads** phase and have begun the interviewing process. By the time the company entered the **Conflict** quadrant, they were ready to make their decisions. The pattern is like a negative downward spiral, which is exponential in nature. Once the employees see that a highly respected, key individual has left amidst all the problems, they know it is time to get their resumes together and start looking. All that remains are the *dead wood* employees who have no place to go. If this problem is not resolved promptly, top management will be relying on the weakest people to bring the business back to good **health**. That is a nearly impossible task. One alternative, of course, is to hire good people. The big problem is that talented people will see that the company is in trouble and will not want to join. If they do not recognize that the company is in trouble, they are probably not the talent level required to help the company. This dilemma is the reason why bringing in new employees generally does not work.

Time is racing on the **Corporate Clock**. The organization needs to work with the people on hand. That is why, at this stage, outside consultants are often brought in. They have the required experience and are familiar with the issues. If they are competent and have established a good track record, you can be sure they have brought many businesses back to good **health** under similar circumstances. But can top management admit they have failed? Will ego, once again, get in the way of saving the company? Since 80% of all companies in the United States fail within ten years, it is safe to assume that, in most cases, ego gets in the way.

By now, it is very obvious that the organization has fallen

apart. The weaker executives are overwhelmed and impotent. The rank and file are acutely aware that there is a lack of leadership at the top. As the *best and the brightest* leave, the business is left with bureaucratic functionaries who are waiting for instructions that will never come.

Top management is often in a state of denial, still hoping that the *good old days* will return. It is common for Kibel Green Issa Inc. to meet with the owner and/or top executive of a business and have him/her spend the first hour telling us how wonderful they are and how well the company is performing. When I was younger, I wondered why they had called me in, since they seemed to have no problems. Then came what I refer to as "the door knob" comment. As I was about to leave, I would be told things like:

- "By the way, we can't make payroll this Friday."

- "We have just been hit with a major suit that could bankrupt the company."

- "I have just lost three of my key executives."

- "Recent sales have dropped by 50%. We are not sure why."

- "The bank has called in the loan. We have 30 days to find a new lender."

- "Many of our major creditors have put us on C.O.D."

- "Our rate of defects is now at 25%, and we can't seem to solve the problem."

- "A new product or competitor has entered the marketplace. They are destroying us."

I would return to the chair in front of the desk and the *real* meeting would begin. I guess the top executive didn't really want me to leave. At the same time, he/she wished I didn't have to be called in.

Our most important task in the **Conflict** phase is to *stop the bleeding*. It may be necessary to offer special incentives to the remaining key people. It is most important that we develop a road map that shows how the company is going to solve its problems. This road map, in the final analysis, must be shared with all entities whose support we need. First, it must be shared with the employees to reassure them and convince them that the company can make it. They must participate in and buy into the solution. Second, it must be shared with the secured lender whose assistance is necessary. In many cases, it also must be shared with key vendors if extended terms will be requested. As the Plan progresses, it is important to keep all these groups informed so they can see that progress is taking place. The remaining talent in the organization must be assessed. A certain amount of reorganization is sometimes necessary to make certain that all the critical functions are led by the best in-house talent available. These actions will also stop the rumors and dramatically improve communication within the organization as well as between the organization, and those entities whose support is desperately needed.

STRATEGIC AND CONTINGENCY PLANNING ARE NON-EXISTENT

Our studies have shown clearly that companies with long-term **health** do Strategic Planning and Contingency Planning as part of their corporate culture. They are always looking ahead, evaluating their capabilities, assessing the current and future competition, and facing the negative risks they may have to encounter. But rather than putting their heads in the sand, they have a specific Plan to deal with each of these potential problems. Of course they intend to enjoy the good times, but they also recognize that long-term **health** requires that they be prepared *in advance* for the bad times.

We have also discovered that none of the companies in **Crisis** ever did Strategic or Contingency Planning, even when business was good. In general, businesses in the **Conflict** stage have not utilized these planning tools. That is why, when confronted with many of the problems we have mentioned already, after a period of further denial, they begin to plan. The planning is done under great pressure with time accelerating. They have lost the ability to implement certain options because the action is too late and the once available monetary and human resources are no longer available. It is hard to plan when so many negative events are occurring. The tendency is to keep putting out the fires, which does buy time. However, if the time is not used effectively, it only delays the inevitable — the slide into the **Crisis** zone.

If there is no Plan and the employees do not understand where the company is headed, they are likely to leave the business. If the vendors believe the business is failing and the bank sees no program, they well may cut off the supply of material and stop lending money. These actions will only accelerate the deterioration process.

I remember meeting with the head of an electronics company. He could not accept his problems. This gentleman had run the company in a dictatorial fashion for many years and was sure that the pure magnitude of his personality would solve his problems. As each problem occurred, he would pour his energy into developing its solution until one day there were more fires than he could handle. Business began to decline. He never did develop a Plan because he thought planning was a waste of time. He did not believe in the 30% rule that I mentioned in earlier chapters. The business ultimately failed because the pressure of trying to hold it together caused him such severe **health** problems that he finally gave up. Since there was no manpower below him, the business could not survive.

I want to spend a moment on the issue of Contingency Planning because I believe it is the secret weapon that businesses with long-term **health** employ. We all recognize that, in a capitalist system, we always will have business cycles. The trick is to survive the lowest portion of the cycle. This can only be accomplished by not over-leveraging the company during the expansion phase. Leveraging is tempting because it maximizes profits in the short run, even though it ensures financial failure in the long run. I believe that a business must be able to absorb a 30% reduction in revenue and still survive. The lost income in the expansion phase will be more than regained by being able to take advantage of opportunities during the down cycle and, more importantly, by surviving.

THE SECURED LENDERS ARE LOSING CONFIDENCE

Now that the business is actually losing money and the deterioration is apparent, the lenders are making plans to protect their position. Our clients often forget that the lender is not an equity investor. No matter how well the business performs, the lenders will earn only their interest. If, however, the business fails, they could lose a portion of their principal. Therefore, they are primarily concerned with their downside risk and want assurances that they will be protected. Top management generally communicates with the secured lender as if the lending institution was a financial participant in the profitability of the business. The bank, more concerned with the underlying assets, may even ask the borrower to secure the debt with specific assets. If the borrower has a personal guarantee, he/she cannot understand why the bank wants specific assets since "they already have everything I own." Unfortunately, we all know that, in desperate times, many owners have given out guarantees freely to multiple creditors.

Therefore, the bank may discover many obstacles when it makes its claim on the assets underlying the guarantee.

Since good information is scarce, the bank often is surprised when the deterioration becomes obvious and accuses the company of withholding information or being out of control. The business, in its anxiety to keep the banks quiet, probably has presented a few plans already and has failed to accomplish any of them. All credibility is lost. The lender no longer will believe the company. As experienced consultants with a long track record, one of our roles is to stabilize the environment by finding out the truth and making certain it is communicated to the secured lender. We, of course, need absolute honesty from the client to accomplish this. They often relent, for it is their only hope for getting the support of the bank.

If, for any reason, the company has acted in an unethical manner, they ultimately will have to leave the bank. These institutions have long memories. Even after we have turned a business around and both the company and the lender have expressed their gratitude, the lender has told us to locate another bank. They don't want to deal with this management again. That's why it is best to tell the truth as early as possible and show the lender how the problem is going to be solved. Then continue to inform the lender of your progress.

Unfortunately, most companies in the **Conflict** phase do not seek help, keep the lenders at bay, and find that the institution is getting ready to call the loan. At a minimum, the bank strongly recommends that management locate a new lender, usually within a 30 to 90 day time frame. Management is beginning to realize that (1) without cash, the company will fail; and (2) the lenders, in the final analysis, are still the best sources of cash. The loan is probably in the process of being transferred to the "Special Asset Group," a kind way of referring to the Workout Department. Their task is to salvage the loan. They have replaced the account executive who says he will put in a good word for you as he disappears from the scene. There is still time for the company to right itself. Although it is losing money, the losses are fairly recent and have not had enough time to do permanent damage. There is also time to repair relationships with the banks, vendors, and customers. Top management first must get through the denial phase and accept full responsibility for the problems. They must decide whether or not it's time to cut back the size of the business. They must implement cost reduction programs now and energize the sales and marketing departments. Time is accelerating, and the breakdown has begun. The only major obstacle is the ego of top management.

There was a time when I assumed that nothing was more important than survival and that the owner of a business in the **Conflict** phase surely would do what was necessary to stay in business. I have discovered, however, that many would rather fail than admit their mistakes and seek the needed advice. Generally, that advice is sought only in the **Crisis** phase when there is no other choice. Some executives who have hired our firm readily admitted (after the company was turned around) that some part of them hoped we would fail. If we failed, it would prove that it was impossible to re-establish **health**. Oh, the price some people are willing to pay just to appear to be right!

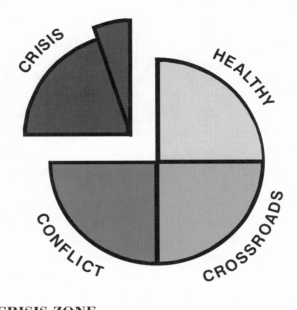

THE CRISIS ZONE

When the **Crossroads** and **Conflict** phases are ignored, a company soon finds itself in **Crisis**. IBM, Johns Manville, Chrysler and scores of other companies that at one time were considered invulnerable found themselves in this situation. At this stage, it is obvious to almost everyone that the ship is sinking, even top management! Only a few folks still wear *rose-colored glasses* and live in a state of permanent denial.

The **Crisis** environment is stressful. The phone is off the hook. In an effort to survive, executives must move at a rapid pace and make enormous strides on a daily basis. They must do the impossible — put out the fires while building a new foundation. It's a schizophrenic existence, having to live in the present and the future at the same time.

Solving problems is expensive and takes a great deal of energy at a time when the organization is strapped for resources. To make matters worse, executives find that *friends* come around less often. In fact, some have disappeared. The feeling of isolation is so powerful that it drains the very energy needed to keep going.

Now the forlorn CEO must seek help and advice in an environment that is not conducive to rational thinking. At this stage, there is only one chance to save the company. An advisor who installs a poor management information system can correct it without threatening the organization, but a turnaround expert must do it right the first time, or all is lost. If the **crisis** is not addressed immediately, there is a **Red Zone** somewhere near 11:55 p.m. on the **Corporate Clock** when it is too late, and there is nothing more to do but liquidate.

Generally, there is not enough time to implement the strategic changes that would have been possible in the **Crossroads** phase. They require too long a lead-time. Nor is there enough time to receive the full benefit of cost reductions. They, too, take time, and there is often an increased need for cash to pay for severance and accrued vacations before savings are realized. The emphasis on profits, which was a guidepost, has now shifted to the management of assets and liabilities, and the most important asset of all — CASH. Our goal in this phase is to convert receivables, inventories, and fixed assets to cash as quickly as possible — EVEN AT THE RISK OF NEGATIVELY IMPACTING THE PROFIT AND LOSS STATEMENT. If you run out of cash, *the ball game is over.* Many executives do not understand this. By now, the bank lines of credit are no longer available, so cash must be generated internally.

While turning converted assets into cash, we also attempt to delay the disbursement of cash by stretching payables and trying to renegotiate debt with the secured lender(s).

Addressing the **Crisis** phase is so complex that I have written a book on the subject, *How to Turn Around a Financially Troubled Company* (McGraw-Hill, 1982), which is used extensively in the workout field.

What does this **Crisis** environment look like?

• Time is accelerating.

- Chaos is everywhere. Good information is hard to find.

- Balance Sheet management is primary in importance.

- Cash is king. It now gets the status it has always deserved.

- Intense leadership effort is required, including 16 to 20 hour days.

- Secured creditors are on your back.

- Unsecured creditors are on your back.

- Lawsuits are both threatened and in motion.

- The *best and the brightest* have left or are leaving.

- Top management desperately needs advisors, yet subliminally hopes the advisors will fail.

- Credibility has been lost with creditors, vendors, customers, employees and shareholders.

- Marriages are falling apart, and health problems rear their heads.

- No sources of capital, in any form, appear to be available.

TIME IS ACCELERATING

By the time a company reaches the **Crisis** quadrant, the effort to survive is enormous. Daily reports are necessary to prevent a disaster. Monthly information, which is generally adequate for a **Healthy** company, is now useless.

Time is accelerating at thirty times the speed of the **Clock** at a **Healthy** company. No wonder executives get *burned out!* It is virtually impossible to deal with all the important issues. Since there is usually a lack of control, some sort of makeshift daily information system must be created. This takes time to create and time to monitor. The cash control system, for example, involves daily meetings with key executives who decide who gets paid, who gets delayed, and who informs the creditors who will be delayed. This takes time. It also takes time to deal with the endless phone calls from unsecured creditors who should not be ignored. At times, it will be necessary to have one-on-one meetings with key creditors. This also takes time. The bank(s) want to meet with you more often and insist that you provide them with plans and up-to-date information. This takes time. Employees clamor to meet with you to find out what's happening and to get your assurance that everything will work out. Key people are resigning. You need to meet with them to try to convince them to stay on some basis. This also takes time. If you are a public company, you have to deal with shareholders and the press. This is very time consuming. Worst of all, none of these activities have anything to do with taking the necessary steps to improve the operations. That is why sixteen to twenty hour days are required. It is hard to drum up that energy when you feel isolated and beaten down, when key employees have left you, and the creditors are questioning your credibility and competence. That time must be invested, and you must show a hopeful face to insiders and outsiders whose support you need in order to survive. In my experience, those leaders with a high survival personality structure make it through the **Crisis**. Others just feel whipped and finally *throw in the towel.*

One dear client of mine called me in at nearly midnight on the **Corporate Clock**. In helping him, my first task was to meet with a major California bank that threatened to call in the loan. We had to do a lot of homework in a hurry, including gaining an understanding of the bank's exposure. The owner of the business had to take a tough stance. At the same time, we had to show the bank that we had at least a preliminary Plan for survival and that they would have substantial exposure if they were to call in the loan at this time. It was a tough meeting, but we came away with an agreement that bought precious time. We used that time effectively, and the company not only turned around, but also became a success. The owner, however, was no stranger to poverty. He was born into it. He was brave and willing to spend whatever time was necessary to survive, and so he did. He has become a friend, and it makes me feel good to know that I assisted in his struggle. Other less hardy executives have failed under the same set of circumstances.

CHAOS IS ALL AROUND, AND GOOD INFORMATION IS HARD TO FIND

When you enter the offices of a business in **Crisis**, you can feel the tension in the air. Tempers are short. Organization is out the window. Everyone is just trying to survive. They hope to get through the day and pray that the next day will be less stressful. But it never is! In fact, the days will become more stressful as time passes. By now, the systems and controls have completely broken down. No one knows what is happening, and everyone is blaming everyone else. People are quitting. It's hard to know what to do first. There is no time for planning. There is hardly enough time to address the problems as they occur. Your accountants also are beginning to worry because they gave you a clean bill of health last year. Now they will be extra careful. This means they will be very conservative and write down everything in sight. This conservative treatment of your financial statements will make the lenders even more upset and cause them to take precipitous action. This is a good example of the "domino" principle in action! In one company, the auditors would allow certain finished goods inventory to be recorded as a sale if the client could specify and provide evidence of the buyer and further demonstrate that the sale probably would occur within ten days. Now these expensive products ($15,000 each) will be treated as inventory. The inconsistency will erode profits even further.

Driven by the outside accountant and demands that top management use conservative accounting, the Chief Financial Officer also tends to get concerned. In one case, the owner refused to listen to the Chief Financial Officer and he went directly to the bank because he was concerned about his future credibility.

Then along come the attorneys, who have a field day! At a time when the company is strapped for cash, it starts receiving enormous legal bills. It must respond to the many lawsuits that are in motion. These come from the creditors and, if there has been a significant reduction in personnel, in the form of wrongful termination cases. At the same time, it generally becomes necessary to hire bankruptcy counsel to begin preparation for a possible filing. If the company actually does file, the professional fees become horrendous. There have been cases when I had to inform a company that they couldn't afford a Chapter 11 filing because they had insufficient funds to pay the professionals!

The secured lender probably has called in the loan and may be taking other legal action against the firm. The bank certainly has transferred the account to the Workout Department, which tends to be less friendly than the account managers.

The company needs a Plan, badly, because everyone wants to know how it is going to get out of this mess. But there is no time to plan. Worst of all, the whole environment is negative. The business is being attacked from all sides. It's been a long time since anyone received a compliment — even at home. The result is chaos. There is no order to the workday. Management focuses on putting out the next fire. Secretly, everyone knows that if there ever can be *light at the end of the tunnel* without *a train coming from the other direction,* there must be a Plan. Putting out fires only delays the time of death. It has no impact on the certainty of it. Is it any wonder that the **Crisis** environment is one of confusion and, in many cases, hopelessness?

THE BALANCE SHEET IS PRIMARY

When I met one of my clients who had once been a successful distributor, he was still talking about how he was going to increase the profitability of his business. He had aggressive plans for increasing sales and reducing costs. The company distributed product to the automotive industry, which looked like it was beginning to improve. How could I tell him that he was too late? In the **Healthy**, **Crossroads**, and probably the **Conflict** quadrants, there would have been time to address the revenue and expense issues. When we spoke, I could see that the company would be out of business in the next 60 to 90 days unless proper action was taken. It was very depressing for the client. He had to put his dreams on hold in order to survive. He was, however, up to the task and took the action necessary to insure that the company would remain viable.

Increasing sales is a slow process, which often involves additional investment before the benefits can be realized. Similarly, the reduction of costs, particularly those related to personnel, involves severance, vacation pay, etc., before the benefits can be realized. The conversion of assets to cash, the extension of liabilities, and the restructuring of debt provide immediate relief, which is essential in the **Crisis** quadrant. Unfortunately, most executives are not familiar with Balance Sheet management. They worry that the sale of obsolete inventory, for example, will have a negative impact on the Profit and Loss Statement. My response is, "So what, if the alternative is to be out of business in ninety days and lose it all!"   The alert executive, at a minimum, must do the following:

- **Accelerate The Collection Of Receivables** — Individuals must be assigned specific accounts, and incentives must be developed to collect the money as quickly as possible.

- **Sell Obsolete Inventory** — Many years ago, when I was running a recreational vehicle company during the energy crisis, we had to sell motor homes as portable housing for the Alaska Pipeline and trailers as portable offices. Neither of these "dinosaurs" could be sold for their original uses at any price. In most companies, the inventory problem may require less imagination, but it may be necessary to take severe *hits* to the Profit and Loss Statement.

- **Sell Fixed Assets** — Often, idle pieces of real estate can be sold. If the company owns certain facilities, it may want to consider a sale and leaseback. If business is down, some equipment may be idle and convertible into cash.

- **Consolidate And Shut Down Facilities** — Even if the asset cannot be sold rapidly, there may be immediate benefits in shutting down a facility or consolidating operations so that they utilize less space.

- **Manage Accounts Payable** — There is an art to getting all of your key creditors to provide extended terms. Done correctly, you can create an immediate source of interest free cash. Handled incorrectly, you can find yourself on C.O.D. with each of them. The secret is to show the creditors that you have a Plan, that their exposure is minimal, and that failure to support you would probably result in a complete write down of their entire balance.

- **Restructure Secured Debt** — Get the bank to provide extensions and deferrals until you can provide them with a Plan that more carefully defines the full restructuring required.

It is interesting to observe that, had top management paid attention to the Balance Sheet when they were in the earlier quadrants, they probably could have avoided the **crisis** in the first place. I believe, with very few exceptions, that it is unnecessary for a business ever to get into a **crisis** if there is vigorous Balance Sheet management built into the corporate culture.

CASH IS KING

The reader may well ask, "Isn't cash just a part of the Balance Sheet? Why do you have to discuss it separately?" The answer is that cash is so important and so underrated by many top executives that it *deserves* its own separate section.

I think the problem begins in school where all emphasis is placed on earnings and revenue. Everyone wants to be *big*. In many cases, size is even more important than profits. Everyone wants their pals at the country club to know that they run a large company. Sales volume is the best measure of that.

When a company is formed, there is an early appreciation of the importance of capital, but once the business passes the start-up phase and feels it is in the **Healthy** zone, all attention switches back to the Profit and Loss Statement. As the business begins to decline and starts its rapid descent into the **Crossroads** or **Conflict** quadrants, the focus is usually on increasing revenue and reducing expenses. **The simple recognition that when you run out of cash, you're out of**

business, often does not reach the top executive's level of awareness until he/she gets into the Crisis phase. As a result, the company generally does not have cash control systems in place that (1) provide for future viability; and (2) assist management in taking *real time* action. Typically, we initiate a Daily Cash Management System to determine who gets paid, when bills get paid, and how to treat those creditors whose payments will be deferred. We also have to install an effective Cash Forecasting System to make certain we do not run out of this precious asset before a turnaround occurs.

One of my clients was in the business of making plastic resin. The company's bank, a major California institution, agreed not to take action if we could provide them with a Plan supported by a Daily Cash Flow System within ninety days. This information would be measured against the previously submitted Plan and would demonstrate how we would get through the period. The real understanding was that, as long as we stayed within the Plan, we would have the ninety days. If there were significant deviation, the bank would call in the loan. In any case, after the ninety-day period, they still might call in the loan if progress was not made or they did not like the Plan!

The bank had misgivings about some of the key management people. We made major organizational changes during that period. We also reduced expenses without affecting revenue — a good start. However, I cannot count the number of reality sessions I had with the owner before it sank in that, without cash, there is no business, no matter how good the Profit and Loss Statement looks. I had to remind him, again, that the bank is not an equity investor. His lender just wanted to make certain that he could pay back the loan.

A major company in the data processing field presented me with a projection that showed they would be out of the woods in nine months. Unfortunately, they would be out of cash in six weeks. I asked the CEO what his plan was to deal with this situation. He shrugged his shoulders and said, "Somehow, we'll make it." I suggested, instead, that we seek some sort of bridge financing, even if we had to pay a higher rate to get it. It was hard work, but bridge financing was arranged, and the company was saved.

PHENOMENAL EFFORT IS REQUIRED ON THE PART OF TOP MANAGEMENT

The **Clock** has come full circle. Time is accelerating at a rapid pace. Fires must be put out. Personnel problems must be addressed. The day-to-day business must be run, and a Plan is needed to avoid disaster. Unsecured creditors and bankers are demanding meetings. There is simply not enough time available in the normal workday.

A few years ago, we were trying to save a major industrial real estate developer. The pressure was intense. The man acted like he was taking drugs, or something! He began to avoid people and phone calls. He could not take the pressure and did not have the stamina to work the long hours and the seven-day weeks. He had to be replaced because he became non-functional. The directing of a successful turnaround takes more than competence. It takes *tenacity*. It takes the kind of people who never let go until they get what they want; who have the egos to withstand repeated rejection, yet go on trying; who can keep the troops motivated while personally being in a depressed state. What is it about a leader who survives this ideal that is different from those who fail? Here are some of my thoughts based on over forty years of experience.

Survivors:

- Have a clear sense of their personal goals and objectives.

- Have a support system that generally includes family, friends (real friends, not business acquaintances), and a value system that works for them.

- Are in good health and have excellent stamina.

- Have well-developed egos that withstand rejection.

- Do not generally use the word "failure."

- Are excellent negotiators. They do not necessarily have to be as strong operationally.

- Are well connected and are not afraid to use their connections.

- Are respected by their creditors and customers.

- Understand what the financial statements are all about.

The traits outlined above are essential. If the top executive does not possess these traits, the best action to take is to recruit replacements who do have them. They may come from within, or outside professionals may have to be hired.

SECURED CREDITORS ARE ON YOUR BACK

There is no rest for the weary in this quadrant. The bank probably has called in the loan by now and may be accusing management of wrongdoing, incompetence or both. You are begging them for more time to work out the situation. The loan is in the Workout Department. That young account executive who said he/she would always be there for you somehow has disappeared A tough-looking, seasoned executive who looks *through you* whenever you meet and is a lot less sympathetic has replaced him. Your account executive has been transferred to another branch or, if responsible for many accounts like yours, is out looking for a job! Each time you ask for an extension, they demand more personal assets to protect the loan. You are somewhat concerned that their next step might be to take your spouse as hostage or ask for rights to your first-born child. You are relieved to discover that they merely want all your assets in addition to the personal guarantee you foolishly signed a long time ago, when it probably wasn't necessary.

The lender, while waiting, will continue to squeeze down the loan balance, changing the lending formula so that less money can be advanced. They may install a "lock box" system to make certain that they receive all the collections. Their Plan is to keep up the pressure until you can't handle any more and you leave. The other option, of course, is Chapter 11 filing. There was a time when the banks worried about filing. Now they simply understand the pros and determine whether or not it is in their best interest to avoid it or to let you file. They will be careful not to interfere with management except to implement those actions required to protect their position as a lender.

You soon discover that you are not bankable. An equity investment would be wonderful, but who would want to invest in a business in **crisis**? There are vulture funds that may try to steal away your business and buy off the bank's loan at a deep discount. A better bet is often the asset-based lenders, if there are enough overall assets at liquidation to secure the loan. They may charge more than five points over prime and request a substantial fee for their due diligence. These lenders often operate in that window where you are not bankable and may go under. If you turn the business around, they realize you probably will return to a bank. If you fail, they know how to liquidate your assets so they can be made whole. The window is often about two years, and the rates are very high. However, they could be the only hope for survival.

I was involved in saving a publicly held computer company that was in serious financial trouble. Its bank was being very aggressive, calling in the loan and claiming that management had done some terrible things that would make a grown man blush. The company had a great Plan, but they would run out of cash before the cash flow and profits could be turned. All the major banks turned them down. We found it necessary to file a Chapter 11 to delay the existing lender's ability to shut the company down immediately. We then located an asset-based lender who moved rapidly to make the loan. Since the loan offered was less than the balance due, we negotiated a payment in full with the bank at less than one hundred cents to the dollar. More importantly, that two-year loan saved the company. We came out of the filing successfully, brought the business back to profitability, and the company became bankable again.

More aggressive positions can sometimes be taken with existing lenders. That information is contained in my first book, *How To Turn Around A Financially Troubled Company*, and is outside the scope of this one.

UNSECURED CREDITORS ARE ON YOUR BACK

The unsecured creditors have a different problem. They can't call in the loan. At best, they may be able to recover some of their inventory but, in general, they must wait behind the secured creditors and pray that, after the professionals get paid, there is something left over. Generally, there is very little left for them. If the creditors cut off all credit, the business surely will fail. If they extend credit, they may increase their exposure. Sometimes creditors prefer a filing because credit advanced after the filing can get a preferred position. A filing, however, often will have enough of a negative effect on the revenue of the business to ensure its failure. Some creditors will put the company on C.O.D. so that the exposure is capped. If used by the major creditors, the C.O.D. may dry up all the available cash rapidly, thereby accelerating the company's demise. One also must be careful about giving preferential treatment to some creditors over others.

It is time to negotiate but, before that, certain important analyses must be performed. First, the allocation of assets to the various classes of creditors must be examined. Oftentimes, this study will show that, upon liquidation, there is little or nothing available for the unsecured creditor. This fact alone might convince the creditors to be more patient and cooperative, but it isn't usually enough. A Plan also must be developed that shows how the company finally survives operationally, if it receives the appropriate support from both the secured and unsecured creditors. The Plan must be believable to the creditors. If there is a workable (feasible) Plan, if the demands are reasonable, and if an acceptable Plan (acceptable to creditors) exists to turn the company around, then there is a good chance that time can be bought through creative negotiation.

At times, I have successfully utilized the Credit Managers Association to work out such a settlement. If the creditors agree to go along with this, it is less expensive than a filing and does not carry the same stigma.

If the company does file, a Creditors Committee (composed of the largest creditors) must be formed. They will have their own attorney, and guess who gets to pay for the Creditors Committee counsel as well as the bankruptcy counsel? You guessed right! *The Debtor pays.*

The Committee will make many demands on you and will be upset when the concessions from the bank are inadequate in their eyes. You will bounce like a tennis ball between the bank and the Creditors Committee, and no one will be satisfied. Welcome to the **Crisis** quadrant.

LAWSUITS ARE THREATENED AND IN MOTION

Out of the woodwork come all of the problems that management was able to maintain control over when the company was perceived as **healthy**. Now *the cat is out of the bag,* and the whole world knows you are in trouble. They want to get money out of you before others get there and nothing is left. Employees who have recently been terminated can sue the company for sexual harassment, wrongful termination, or failure to meet implied or written contractual obligations. Unsecured creditors will sue for the amounts due them. They may try to take back their goods and get their hands on first moneys by means of an attachment. The secured creditors are less likely to sue unless they have evidence there has been wrongdoing on the part of top management or the ownership. Shareholders may feel they have been misled by management and begin to take action. If this is a public company, you could be faced with a class action lawsuit. There are attorneys who spend all of their time studying businesses whose stock has fallen dramatically since the public offering. When they select a target company, they notify the shareholders, whom they expect to be unhappy, and begin the process. One common technique is comparing the Board minutes of a company with its press and shareholder releases to see if there has been full disclosure. Few firms will survive this scrutiny unscathed. One high tech company in Southern California had to pay off a multi-million dollar settlement even though, I am certain, there was no wrongdoing. Law firms intend to build up enough of a circumstantial case to insure that the company will settle.

Once there is a failure to make lease payments on time, the landlords will begin to take legal action to protect their interests. The legal and accounting fees increase dramatically because of the need to defend the company. This happens at precisely the time when the business is trying to reduce its costs.   Customers start returning goods because they are beginning to purchase from sources that they perceive will be around in the future. Accounts Receivable also slow down, and customers make all sorts of claims related to quality, accuracy of the balance, etc. in order to delay or avoid payment. The company has to engage counsel to go after these people, thereby incurring additional legal expenses. As you can see, the **Crisis** quadrant follows a downhill spiral that must be stopped as quickly as possible.

THE BEST AND THE BRIGHTEST ARE LEAVING

The world comes crashing down, and one needs all the help one can get. The acceleration of time makes it impossible for any one person to manage all the problems. A great effort is required to address legal matters, which are very time consuming. The business still must be run and will not wait. The various fires that ignite must be put out immediately, or the company will be consumed. The best and most marketable employees are also the brightest, and they can see that the business is on the verge of failing. They also know that, if they stay around and are associated with the failure, it may be hard to find work in the future. Unless they have developed a fierce loyalty to the business, they will be among the first to leave. Sometimes they can be encouraged to stay by providing financial incentives, but this usually doesn't work because they can't be paid enough to offset their perception of long-term damage to their careers.

One of my clients was in the business of converting film to tape and the coloration of black and white movies. This company found itself in the **Crisis** zone. When we arrived, we discovered a complete lack of experienced management reporting to the new top executive. In effect, this executive had no talent to assist him. It would be difficult to hire talent because skilled people would not want to join such a company. Hence the need for hands-on outsiders to get the job done. The new executive was beside himself, but rapid loss of talent in the **Crisis** quadrant is common.

AMBIVALENT FEELINGS EXIST TOWARD ADVISORS

Another client was a well-known manufacturer of high tech equipment. I was brought in to help save his company. I needed to know everything about the business, including all the *skeletons in the closet,* yet he withheld important information that could make me fail. He knew that the latest financial statement would show a larger than expected loss. I was scheduled to meet with his banker to try to arrange for some extension of credit. I was informed that the statements were not ready, but that they would probably show a breakeven for the month. After working out an interim arrangement with the bank, in good faith, the financials were finally released a few weeks later. A rightfully angry bank wondered if I was in collusion with my client to get an agreement signed before releasing the bad news. If I did not have a well-established rapport with the institution, the client would have rendered me useless for the purpose of all future negotiations. Once the credibility of the advisor is destroyed, he/she can't help anymore. I used to wonder why clients often sabotaged their consultants. It didn't make sense. After all, they wanted to survive, and the consultant's task was to help make that happen. Isn't survival the highest need? The answer is a resounding **"no."** There is an even greater need and that is the protection of the ego. The client has spent months, and possibly years, trying to save a business, which seems to be failing. What does it say about competence if an outside consultant can come in and turn the company around in a short period of time even though he is less familiar with the nature of the business? Whereas, if the consultant fails, it proves that no one could have saved the business, and the failure was not due to poor management. Does this logic blow your mind? It did mine when I was less experienced, but now I understand that this need to defend one's ego operates at a very deep level. Often, the client is not aware that he is destroying his own chances for survival. That is why I now hold closed door, one on one meetings in which I address management with the whole *chamber of horrors* and the usual *skeletons in the closet*. I use a checklist. While some of my questions may be embarrassing, it gets the job done. I also inform clients that if they have done anything unethical or illegal, I will drop their case immediately.

Throughout the course of an engagement, experienced consultants recognize that clients will vacillate between seeing you as an ally and treating you as an enemy who is out to destroy their reputation. They wonder if they should confide in you. They know that if you are working with only half of the information, you probably will fail. Yet, they will withhold. I have often told the professionals in my firm that, upon completion of a workout engagement, they have probably earned a degree in psychology.

CREDIBILITY IS LOST AT ALL LEVELS

It is a lonely feeling to be running a business that is failing. At home, spouses may be nervous. If the marriage is a good one, the spouse is concerned about health. If the marriage is a bad one, the spouse is concerned about the economic impact on lifestyle and status in the community. Since over half of all marriages are not good, the top executive feels pressure and loss of prestige at home.

At the office, the other employees who previously looked up to their leader are no longer certain about leadership's capability. After all, it was their leader who led the company into the **Crisis** quadrant. This is definitely a credibility problem.

The bank has now received the company's latest Plan for survival. Many Plans have been submitted before, and none of them worked. Why should they believe this Plan? They believe the company is lying or incompetent. Either way, they would like this company out of their bank. Trust has been violated. Close contacts at the bank have disappeared from the scene and, while some of them may cheer from the sidelines, one senses that they also are questioning credibility. It is a tough psychological environment for seeking another bank or trying to restructure debt with an existing bank.

Shareholders are now asking tough questions. Board meetings are downright unpleasant, and Board oversight activities have increased dramatically. Board members question the CEO's command of facts and strategic decisions. It is evident that they would replace this executive if they had the power. Some of those whom the CEO previously thought were business buddies are, somehow, too busy for lunch or dinner plans. Credibility is disappearing rapidly. The CEO begins to question his/her own abilities.

Customers have heard rumors, fueled by competitors, that the business is failing. When they see the payables slowing down, they take it as a sign of trouble. It is an easy step for them also to question management's abilities. The customers begin to hear "badmouthing" from the sales and marketing departments. Soon the *self-fulfilling* prophecy begins to do its work. Customers, knowing that there are problems, begin to look to other sources, and revenue starts to decline.

Finally, we have a credibility problem with the unsecured creditors who are the critical source of supply that enables a company to conduct business. They have not been paid on time. Payment promises have been made and not kept, and they no longer believe the company. Credibility is lost, yet in this environment, someone is expected to save the business.

MARRIAGE AND HEALTH PROBLEMS APPEAR

What more could happen to the strife torn executive than living the dreadful scenario described above? Alas, there is more to come. Marriages, as described earlier, are falling apart. Often divorce proceedings are already in motion. The stress level at home is as great if not greater than that in the office. In addition to all the business related attorneys described in other sections of this book, bankruptcy counsel appear on both sides. If the spouse is angry, the attorney is apt to attack like a barracuda who will not be happy until financial destruction prevails — as if there weren't enough problems already!

The level of stress can reach dangerous proportions and often leads to serious health problems. In one major workout, we had a tense meeting with a banker. The client was so incensed at the banker's accusations that he leaned across the table and decked the bank's Senior Vice President. I had to act as a referee to make certain no one was badly hurt. The client had a heart attack the very next day and died.

I have often said that a divorce attorney and a cardiologist could make a fortune following our firm around when we perform workouts! It is a sad commentary on our society. I observe that many marriages are based on the economic well-being of the breadwinner. There are few real friends, so in time of need, the support system is not there. I believe it is that support system which reduces stress and keeps the top executive in balance so that there is sufficient energy available to complete the turnaround. It is as important for executives to know how to meditate and relax as it is to address business issues. They must confront the real problems and guard against *rearranging the chairs on the Titanic.*

Most executives do not have a balanced set of goals in their lives. Therefore, their entire identity revolves around their economic and business stature (or perceived stature). When I find executives in the **Crossroads** or **Conflict** quadrants, I recommend that they consider establishing a broader range of goals for themselves. Their self worth must go beyond business alone. If it doesn't, they have no other sense of self worth to help them through the **Crisis** phase without doing great damage to themselves, both physically and psychologically.

SOURCES OF CAPITAL APPEAR TO BE UNAVAILABLE

Your existing lender called in your loan. You have a limited amount of time to find new sources. Since you are losing money and the business is deteriorating, this will not be an easy task. The traditional sources, such as banks that tend to lend based on cash flow as well as asset support, are no longer available to you. These are the sources with which you are most familiar.

You begin to look at asset-based lenders. They are an option only if you have sufficient assets to collateralize your loan. Asset-based lenders typically value your assets at liquidation and often take an additional twenty percent cushion. If the assets of the business and the personal assets you can contribute are insufficient, these sources also become unavailable. Asset-based lenders will charge a much higher rate of interest than banks, will require guarantees, and will manage their loan with greater controls. They are not afraid to liquidate, and the threat of a filing does not create much concern. That is their business. You either survive and leave them or fail and get liquidated.

If the business is in trouble but still has an excellent future, equity capital may be the best alternative. It may become necessary to give up a large portion of the equity of the business to raise this capital. At times, it may become necessary to give up control of the business. There are funds that specialize in investing in troubled companies. Of course, they will extract a pound of flesh before completing the transaction, but they can move quickly. Private sources may also be available. They are harder to find, but they, too, can move rapidly if they are interested. At times, it is possible to raise capital from multiple sources through a partnership structure, but you need sufficient lead time to put the disclosure information together. When a business is in the **Crisis** phase, there is usually very little time for this kind of preparation.

The alert top executive would have been cultivating sources of capital while the business was doing well. He/she would have met the heads of these workout funds and would have played golf or tennis with the major asset-based lenders in town. He/she would have a cadre of wealthy individuals who have expressed an interest in investing. Then, if a problem occurs, he/she could go right to these sources and get a prompt response. I suspect, however, if the top executive were the type to have developed these sources in the good times, he/she would not be likely to get into the **Crisis** zone in the first place.

In spite of all I have said in this chapter, I have found that many top executives are wearing *rose-colored glasses* when I first meet them. They are still in a state of extreme denial. They have convinced themselves that the problem will blow over, or they simply deny that it exists. Unless I can get the executive to face the situation through our one-on-one *reality* sessions, it is impossible to complete the turnaround successfully. These *reality* sessions often include confessions and, in some cases, even some crying in private. But this must happen for the process to move forward. Once an executive believes that there is a solution, *a way out* if you will, hope is renewed, and the organization is ready for *action*.

After reading this chapter, taking the test, and completing a comprehensive analysis, you have located your company's position on the **Corporate Clock**. You know what time it is at your company. Why is this important? Is this just an intellectual exercise or does it have practical applications? I believe a medical analogy is useful at this juncture. If you were perfectly **healthy**, an annual physical (the **health** check) is all you need to ensure that you are still **healthy**. If that **health** check revealed some minor problems (mild obesity, allergies, back problems, etc.), you would be asked to take corrective action such as diet, exercise or medication. Over a period of time, the problems would either disappear or come under control. If the **health** check revealed more serious problems, but nothing life threatening, you would take action sooner to solve the problem (**Conflict** phase). If, however, you were told you had cancer or a serious heart condition, you would immediately start some form of treatment, which could involve chemotherapy, radiation, or surgery. There would be no time to sit around and ponder. You would know that the longer you wait, the less your chances of survival. You would find the best professional talent available to solve your problem.

For an organization to stay **healthy**, it must go through the same process. Yet, organizations composed of many such people do not see their company's **health** problems in the same way. They generally avoid annual checkups (the cheapest approach in the long run) for fear that something will be wrong. If something *is* wrong, no matter how severe, there is a tendency to deny that the problem exists. Perhaps the difference is that the death of a company does not carry the same element of fear as does the death of an individual. It is true, however, that failed companies often destroy lives. Many people become physically ill, are psychologically shattered or impoverished. A number of individuals who relied on pension plans now find they have nothing to fall back on, and they are too old to rebuild their asset base.

As with an individual, if company problems are caught early and acted upon, they usually can be solved. This dynamic process must continue throughout the life of a business, just as physical examinations are important throughout a person's life.

Once you know the quadrant that you are in, you know how you must deal with a given problem. The general rules are as follows:

- **HEALTHY** — Take your time, analyze problems carefully, consider the long-term impact. Then implement the corrective action in an orderly fashion. Continue to check your **health** annually to make certain your business remains in the **Healthy** quadrant.

- **CROSSROADS** — There is less time to fix problems, but they can be remedied. Often a simplified system has to be installed because there isn't enough time to design and implement a sophisticated system. Once the organization has moved back into the **Healthy** quadrant, upgrade the system.

- **CONFLICT** — There is generally only enough time for a *Band-Aid* solution. Just get at the high priority aspects of the problem. There is not enough time to solve the problem completely. Solving problems that do not provide short-term benefits must be avoided or your resources may be consumed by low priority problems.

- **CRISIS** — The patient may be terminal. The approach is *ready, fire, aim!* There is no time for comprehensive analysis. One must act and hope that good decisions are made. Only urgent problems can be addressed in this quadrant. There is no time for anything else.

Before giving specific examples of how the above rules are applied, let me identify some basic concepts that apply as a business accelerates from **Healthy** to **Crisis**. While these concepts are general in nature, I believe they are a good starting point for deciding what needs to be done in addressing a given problem in a given quadrant.   As an organization moves around the **Clock**:

- We concentrate on Balance Sheet management instead of the Profit and Loss Statement.

- Time accelerates from the **Healthy** quadrant until it is thirty times greater in a **Crisis**, conflicting with our idea of linear time.

- Studies, designs of systems, and orderly analysis are replaced by direct action, albeit at the expense of being thorough and careful. There is simply not enough time to address problems in a comprehensive manner.

- The *best and the brightest* are leaving the company, and the general talent level continues to decline.

- The level of denial continues to increase.

- All of the management and infrastructure weaknesses begin bursting out of the closet. The closet door can never be closed again.

- Orderly planning becomes a luxury because more and more time must be spent putting out fires and keeping the ship afloat.

HOW TO HANDLE THE SAME PROBLEMS IN SUBSEQUENT ZONE

Below are just a few examples to emphasize that solutions are related to both the problem being solved and the company's position on the **Corporate Clock**:

Cash Control

When a **healthy** company feels that its cash control system is no longer adequate, it redesigns the system. The system may no longer work because the business has grown significantly, changed, or become more complicated. Since there is no actual cash problem, the new controls can be installed in an orderly manner. If a need exists for long-term cash because of growth, there is time to meet with lenders to expand the lines of credit or to consider various ways to raise additional capital.

In the **Crossroads** quadrant, there is also time, but it is useful to implement some modified *Band-Aid* system. Actual cash needs to be controlled and, while a better system is the answer, cash drain must be addressed promptly. Preparations also should begin as soon as possible for meetings with the lender. They need to know that the company has a problem and may need some short-term cooperation. The key here is not to surprise the bank. There is little need to inform anyone else.

In the **Conflict** stage, the *Band-Aid* system must be implemented as quickly as possible. Asset collection needs to be accelerated, while liabilities need to be extended. In other words, collect receivables and drag payables. The bank needs to be notified soon, before they find out the hard way, i.e., non-monetary defaults on your loan agreements or failure to meet the monetary requirements of the loan on time.

Make sure that, at a minimum, some sort of Cash Flow Plan, is developed before the meeting, with some explanation of how the company got into trouble in the first place. The Plan also should show the bank how the company is going to get out of its dilemma and return to the **Healthy** quadrant. Let the bank know that a more comprehensive Plan is being developed, but start maximizing cash flow internally.

In the **Crisis** quadrant, it is too late to even think about designing systems. The only system that works is daily cash control to make certain that no unnecessary disbursements are made. Cash must be marshalled in every way possible. Receivables must be accelerated. It may be necessary to give incentives to creditors to accelerate their payments. Vendors must be delayed mercilessly to the extent they will allow without cutting the company off or putting it on C.O.D.

Inventory

When a **Healthy** company has an inventory problem, management hires experienced systems people to design a comprehensive inventory control program that considers safety stock, reorder points, economic order quantities, cube considerations, etc. Once the system is designed, the Purchasing, Warehouse, and Inventory Control Managers are trained to use the information. There is initial resistance and some modification may be necessary but, in time, the system will prove to work. The company receives the long-term benefits of minimizing the amount of capital tied up in inventory. This, in turn, releases working capital that can be used more productively in the creation of profits.

In the **Crossroads** quadrant, there is only time for a modified *Band-Aid* system. It is necessary to study the inventory in a more focused manner. One possible option is establishing controls over the fast moving items and developing a program for disposing of the slow moving inventory. A careful review of the warehouse configuration may also be useful in controlling the flow of product.

In the **Conflict** stage, we need to implement the sale of the old inventory and convert it to cash as soon as possible. There is little time to install any sort of control system. In fact, it may be faster to physically review the inventory and make decisions on the spot.

If the company finds itself in the **Crisis** quadrant, there is no time for any of the niceties. If it runs out of cash, it is out of business. It becomes necessary to sell anything that can be quickly converted into cash in order to buy time. There is no time for any systems analysis. It is time to move "full speed ahead" and "damn the torpedoes."

Real Estate And Fixed Assets

In the **Healthy** and **Crossroads** quadrants, it is generally not necessary to be aggressive in terms of real estate and fixed assets. Idle equipment and real estate should, of course, be converted into cash. (Hopefully, real estate is not owned at the corporate level.)

In the **Conflict** quadrant, the company should try to minimize its usage of square footage and either sublease, sell, or renegotiate the lease with the landlord. If cash is tight, a sale and leaseback should be considered seriously for all owned assets.

In the **Crisis** quadrant, the situation changes dramatically. All idle assets must be sold as soon as possible. One cannot wait to get the best price. If space is made available, it should be subleased as soon as possible. Idle equipment should be sold as well. The company must try to complete a sale and leaseback of all company owned property.

Organizational Problems

At this point, the relationship between the problem, the solution and the company's place on the **Corporate Clock** should be clear. In the earlier quadrants, management would perform an organizational study and develop the structure required to meet its strategic needs. A series of organization charts would be created showing the step-by-step transitions that are required to achieve company goals. Detailed organization charts would be developed spelling out each position with its responsibility, authority and reporting relationship. The Plan would be implemented in an orderly manner with sensitivity to the needs of employees. Care would be exercised to avoid charges of wrongful termination and the like.

However, as we move from **Conflict** into **Crisis**, the situation changes. Personnel must be reduced; costs must be reduced, and there isn't enough time for careful planning. The top executives seek the best professional advice they can get, but there is a need to act quickly. Mistakes may be made, but the mistake of not surviving is unacceptable.

After reading this chapter, I suggest that the goal of long-term **health** will be achieved if you adhere to the program in the following outline:

- Conduct an Operations Review. A cancer could be growing, even though the surface appears **healthy**.

- Determine where the company is on the **Corporate Clock** on an overall basis and by key functions.

- Identify, in detail and by function, the tasks that must be accomplished to return the function, and ultimately the company, to the **Healthy** quadrant.

- Assign responsibilities for each project within each function, including appropriate time lines. Control the projects until they are completed successfully.

- Remeasure to confirm the company has moved back to the **Healthy** quadrant.

Over time, there will be fewer and fewer projects, and the company's position on the **Clock** can be determined easily. This program is analogous to personally controlling one's physical health.

THE OPERATIONS REVIEW

Over the past decade, Kibel Green Issa Inc. has developed a comprehensive questionnaire to:

- Improve the client's operating and financial performance;

- Improve the client's Contingency Planning;

- Assist directors in their ability to exercise their fiduciary and social responsibilities;

- Provide a baseline evaluation of financial performance, operations and management practices; and

- Establish this baseline evaluation for comparison in succeeding Operations Reviews.

This Operations Review is very comprehensive but must be tailored to a specific company and industry each time it is used. In addition to an evaluation of the company and industry as a whole, areas covered include: Sales; Marketing; Distribution; R&D/New Products; Manufacturing; Finance; Accounting, Budgeting and Management Reporting; Planning; Personnel; Risk Management; Facilities; EDP; and Contingency Planning.

The Review is designed to leave no stone unturned. It seeks to establish the relative **health** of each major function and, simultaneously, to identify those projects necessary to bring the function and the overall company back to the **Healthy** quadrant. The length of the review is, of course, determined by the size and complexity of the company.

DETERMINE WHERE EACH FUNCTION IS AND WHERE THE COMPANY IS ON THE CORPORATE CLOCK

The first output would be an evaluation of each major function and a determination of its relative **health**. Some functions may be healthier than others. This output is similar in form to undergoing a physical examination. The exam is necessary to understand the **health** issues. It is a necessary step, but **it will not make you healthy**. Good **health** requires that you take action to address your problems. If you are overweight, you must diet. If your cholesterol is high, you must reduce fat intake and, possibly, take medication. If your blood pressure is too high, you may have to learn how to reduce stress in your life, exercise more and, perhaps, take medication. Good **health** is constant work. You need to undergo physical examinations periodically to see if the actions you've taken produced the proper results.

IDENTIFY THE TASKS REQUIRED TO RETURN TO GOOD HEALTH

The same is true of a company. If the Operations Review reveals that proper correction for a high inventory is the installation of an inventory control system, then a system must be installed, and the inventory turnover must be increased. These facts will be revealed in the information system and the next Operations Review. If the information system is not accurate or timely, a new system must be designed. If a business does not do any Strategic Planning or Contingency Planning, they must begin to implement such processes and fine-tune them until they produce the desired results.

ASSIGN RESPONSIBILITIES AND TIME LINES

Once each project is defined, responsibility must be assigned along with committed due dates. The projects then must be followed carefully. It is our experience that, in the first Operations Review, about twenty to thirty key projects are identified. If the company diligently follows this program, the number of key projects declines by nearly 70% after the first year and is minimal after three years. The projects should be objective and clearly stated so that the results can be measured. If we are anticipating a cost reduction in a certain function, the magnitude must be determined, and a system must be in place to measure the results.

REMEASURE AND CONFIRM

In the first year, there is often a brief re-check after the first six months. It may be hard for management to change their habits. Therefore, a re-check can be quite useful. By the second year and certainly by the third year, the business performs the Operations Reviews on its own. It becomes a part of the corporate culture because, once a company experiences the benefit of heightened sensitivity to their corporate **health**, they never want to lose it. In our experience, all **healthy-healthy** companies experience long-term **health**. In one form or another, they are not afraid to measure, correct and remeasure. It is a lifelong process, just like the maintenance of your personal **health**.

I hope this chapter has opened a window of understanding for the reader. Long-term **health** can be achieved. Companies that survive the ups and downs of the economy over long periods of time are not merely lucky. They work hard and remain ever diligent to the endless task of moving each and every key function back into the **Healthy** quadrant.

Unattended, they will drift into **Crossroads** and, if still unattended, move through the **Conflict** phase directly into **Crisis**. This chapter, taken seriously, will ensure that yours is not one of the many companies in the United States that fail within a ten-year period.

Chapter 4

The Impact Of The Technology Revolution On Value Creation

It is absolutely critical for business executives today to understand the dramatic impact of technology — not only because of the opportunities that are created, but also for their very survival. The rate of change is awesome! The prior industrial revolution created empires in telephones, electricity and automobiles. While many of these technologies were invented in the late 1800s, it wasn't until after 1914 that the manufacturing industry began utilizing the assembly line for mass production. This revolution created the vast percentage of what we today call the Fortune 500.

The real question is, "How many of these companies will be in the Fortune 500 once the current industrial revolution is in full swing?" As these outmoded industries begin to fail, we will see a great deal of confusion in the marketplace. Many will sit on their hands waiting for the *good old days* to return.

Others will read the future incorrectly and fail. A few will see the opportunity and embrace the future. These few, in time, will become the new industry leaders.

This revolution is quite different from the last. Change is occurring at record speed. This was not the case in the last industrial revolution. Radar was invented in 1887 but was not in production until 1933 — 46 years later. Television was invented in 1907 but was not on the market until 1936 — 29 years later. The helicopter, invented in 1904, was not available until 1936 — 32 years later. Yet the transistor, which was invented in 1940, was in production by 1950 — 10 years later. It took a mere seven years for 25% of American households to use the Internet. Computers, in the stores since the late 1980s, are being used by 45% of U.S. households, up from 10% a few years ago. It is estimated that 90% of households will have a PC in the near future. As the information age continues and more companies get on the *highway,* it is increasingly difficult to know who your future competitors will be. Barnes and Noble expected to be competing with B. Dalton and Walden Books — *NOT* Amazon.com. Many retailers today find they are caught in a trap. They either can go to catalogue and Internet selling and cannibalize themselves, or lose the business to others. "What is going on here?" you may ask.

This brings us to the second difference in this industrial revolution. The last one was primarily focused on improving the efficiency of the manufacturing process. Mass production created low-priced goods that could be purchased by the mass market. Automobiles were originally toys for the rich, then became affordable to a large segment of the population. The early Dumont black and white 17" television set cost over $500. Today you can buy a color set with a larger screen for significantly less. As a result, almost every American household has a television set.

The current revolution is focused on marketing and distribution. Therefore, determining who will be your next competitor is becoming much more complicated.

Let us first discuss the technological trends over this next decade, then try to understand what impact they will have on business and the opportunity to create value.

THE TECHNOLOGY TRENDS

1. **Fiber Optics And Satellite Systems** — The demand for the Internet will proceed at a rapid pace and will require dramatic changes to handle the huge volume of activity. We currently use ISDN phone lines, ATM phone lines, wireless cable, cable modems, and direct satellite broadcast. Companies should expect to see major technological changes in this area. The bandwidth problem is the key limitation to the information revolution.

   Fiber optics and low orbit satellites, which are expensive today, will become economically feasible when we have mass utilization of personal computers. Fiber can carry an immense quantity of data, but it is very expensive to install. Fiber optics are installed in specific locations. Satellite communication will be more useful outside the major urban areas.   It is expensive to launch, but can be used for both fixed and mobile locations. In the future, fiber optics probably will be utilized in stationary urban areas, while satellite applications (both low orbit and very low orbit) will be used in less dense and in mobile applications.

   The PCS or personal communications systems are useful for low bandwidth fixed and mobile applications because it is less expensive to install smaller digital cellular transmission towers that provide high voice quality. Many joint ventures with major companies already have been formed to address the issue of fiber optics and satellites. They are, no doubt, the solution to the capacity problem. When they come on board, they will make ISDN, ATM, cable modems and the like obsolete. Companies must pay attention to this fact as they plan for the future.

2. **Bandwidth And I^2** — The typical user of the Internet is still using an analog modem running at 28,000 or 56,000 bits per second (bandwidth) via a phone (twisted pair) line. The advent of relatively inexpensive DSL, 600,000 bits per second, for home use improves the quality of the experience but is extremely limited. The problem is that the number of bits that can be passed through the circuits is restricted in two ways. First, even if we could give everyone DSL speeds, the bandwidth is still too narrow. As an example, it would take almost 3 hours to download a 1.5 hour movie. In other words, the best you could hope for is 15 frames per second (fps) or half the viewable rate of 30 fps. (That same movie would take over 2 days at 28.8 thousand bits per second (Kbps) or over 1 day at 56 Kbps.) Second, even if you could give everyone DSL speeds, structurally, the current Internet cannot handle the volume of information. Hence, everyone would be slowed down to 56 Kbps at most.

   Just replacing the current wires with fiber or satellite systems will help but not solve the underlying structural problem. Internet two or I^2 is currently under construction, with parts of it now being used by universities, government agencies and the like (just like Internet was before becoming popular). The speeds of I^2 will bring a major paradigm shift. To give you some idea of the magnitude, on I^2, the 1.5 hour movie we were discussing above, would take 9 seconds.

   If you couple this incredible bandwidth with high quality, true security and virtually unlimited addresses (1,000 addresses for every square meter on our planet) you will have a communications infrastructure that boggles the imagination. You can have real time point-to-point video streaming. Suppose you want to check traffic; there can be a camera at every intersection as well as at every on/off ramp. Imagine having portable video phones, virtual conferences, unlimited movies on demand, virtual shopping that will mimic the shopping experience, and the like.

Companies that are or may look successful utilizing the current Internet system may be at risk once I^2 becomes widely available.

3. **Smart Cards Are Just Around The Corner** — In the near future, we will have a wallet-sized card that will hold all of the data about ourselves. It will be able to interact with any digital device without our intervention. These cards will contain insurance information, legal documents such as your will, financial information, credit cards, medical data, medications, etc. Information will be accessible to businesses in a convenient form and eliminate complicated paperwork. It will no longer be necessary to fill out all those forms to get admitted into a hospital. Is this good . . . is this bad? Does it further erode our privacy? Yes! Nevertheless, will it happen? Yes!

Smart cards will eliminate long check in lines at the airport, speed up admittance to the hospital, and, in general, dramatically reduce the overhead of many businesses to such a degree that it will be a necessary part of our life. I personally do not look forward to experiencing this change. It will replace all those cards we currently carry and reduce the amount of time we spend personally on administrative matters.

4. **Voice Activation** — IBM and Microsoft, along with other companies, have developed the preliminary software capable of responding to voice commands.

Soon it will not be necessary to be a good typist to use the computer. In the near future, we will be able to tell the computer what to do through a series of voice commands. This capability is probably only a few years off. Voice activation will go a long way toward making the computer friendly to a larger segment of the population and will help to accelerate the mass use of technology.

5. **Video Conferencing** — As we increase the bandwidth, we will be able to experience live action video. Businesses with offices across the country and around the world will be able to see and hear each other in real time. This will avoid the many costly and time-consuming trips that are made for a one to two hour meeting. It will enable management to get a lot more done in less time.

   On a personal level, this capability will open many doors. People will be able to consult with experts from around the world in every field without having to travel. It will be easier to shop for products (that do not require direct interaction) because you can see the merchandise and interact with competent people who are not just salespeople. You can view potential vacation areas directly on the Internet to help make family decisions. However, I must point out that this will have a negative impact on air travel, business use of hotels, and the sale and rental of videos. Some win and some lose in this new industrial revolution.

6. **Customized Software** — In the future, more and more software will be designed using object oriented programming wherein modules of code called *objects* are developed to perform specific functions. This rapidly increases the rate at which software can be developed. It makes it possible to produce customized applications for the home and office economically. Object oriented

languages like "small talk" are one of the most important innovations in connectivity.   These traveling
software programs can run any computer and communicate with any operating system. Object languages also
will make it easier for businesses to install new computer systems that are compatible with their existing ones.
By accessing the information and programs according to
current demands, they can leverage the network. This
technology will enable companies to meet the specific
needs of a given customer more quickly. In effect, the
customer will drive the system. Standardization will be
less important. The last industrial revolution promoted
efficiency by delivering standardized products to customers and marketing these products to create a need.
The ability to innovate software programs more easily
could impact some of the software leaders of today.

7. **Home And Portable Computers For The Mass
   Market** — The Internet is the accelerator that will pro-
   pel the use of home and portable computers forward.
   Systems, which are a sophisticated integration of communication and data processing hardware and software,
   will be at the heart of the Internet. Once all this is available, Internet commerce will be a reality. It is not far off.
   As soon as the more powerful customized computer
   appliances are in place, consumers will move on to the
   information highway en masse. Smart software will pull
   the information out of the Internet in accordance with
   our preferences. This will replace the current system of
   searching and clicking. The Internet will become a simple tool to use. As previously mentioned, since the
   1980s, computers have moved into 45% of American
   households. They will be in 90% of households in the
   next seven or so years. Cellular phones have moved into
   the mainstream along with portable laptop and desktop
   systems. We will finally see low cost Internet devices hit

the market. Affordability will not be a problem for most of the population. Once all of the above happens, the revolution will be in its final phases, and a new set of winners and losers will appear. Make sure your business is not one of the losers.

8. **Embedded Microprocessors In Basic Home Appliances** — Over the next decade, we will see the introduction of inexpensive devices that will perform specialized tasks. Technical expertise will not be required because embedded microprocessors will simply *do the right thing*. An example is the palm-sized computer, which simply organizes your appointments, keeps track of addresses, phone numbers, and important events; maintains reminders and planning information; and interfaces with your computer to keep you current and to insure that information will not be lost.

Web TV is another example. It is a simple setup that works with your television set and enables you to access the Internet and exchange e-mail. It will be as easy to use as the television set and, in time, will help accelerate the mass market use of the Internet.

HOW DO ALL OF THESE CHANGES AFFECT BUSINESS AND VALUE CREATION?

1. **Globalization** — The changes described above will occur throughout the world at different rates. This will create an additional opportunity through globalization. The new technology will make globalization possible for mid-market companies. Globalization will no longer be in the exclusive domain of the major corporations. I^2 will also reduce the cost of entry dramatically. We can expect the high tech applications to emerge first in Western Europe, Japan, Australia and New Zealand,

Taiwan, Singapore, Hong Kong, South Korea and Israel. The United States will lead the way. The expansion will be further fueled by the coming of age of the Baby-Boomer generation. Japan will be one of the few countries in this category that will not benefit from the Baby Boomers because its population is aging at a rapid rate. The combination of low birth rates, longevity, and a policy that does not allow immigration will result in a dramatic reduction in the overall population of Japan. As a result, Japan may not receive the full benefit of its emergence as a high tech nation.

The developing nations such as China and Eastern Asia, South America and Eastern Europe will be in the process of completing aspects of the first industrial revolution — producing standardized products for mass consumption. They will move through this phase rapidly because they will learn from the more developed countries. These nations will begin to develop a middle class that will be looking to increase consumption. This creates another opportunity for the mid-size businesses of the United States.

It seems obvious to me that the developing nations must establish free market economies, make major investments in infrastructure, and create more stable democratic political systems. Infrastructure building will call upon skills in designing industrial manufacturing facilities and building roads, highways, airports, etc.

Every company needs to study the rest of the world and identify areas where their *core competencies* can be utilized. This can create an opportunity for enormous growth and higher profit margins. It also can dramatically increase the actual and perceived value of a business.

2. **The Middle Man — A Dying Breed** — The new technology will allow producers to communicate more

effectively with consumers. Real estate brokers, travel agents, car salesman and the like will all be threatened. When a customer wishes to purchase a large ticket item, he/she may contact the company directly. If the product is standard, the customer places the order and the desired product is shipped directly to him/her. Customers who are not certain about their order will be put in touch with an experienced customer representative who can guide them through the purchase and help specify what they desire. The few products that require touching and feeling can be handled by directing the customer to a center where they can see the products and talk with a live customer representative. I believe the younger generation, as they move into the mainstream, will do more online ordering without visiting these centers. Like the outstanding catalogue companies, Internet companies will allow the customer to return merchandise that is not suitable to them, thereby further reducing the need to see the product live. As we introduce the wide bandwidth, customers will be able to see the product in motion on the Internet and listen to a discussion about it by an expert. In time, it will be possible to have an online conversation with a customer representative, further negating the need to visit a center.

If the product is not standard and is low-priced, you would not order directly from the producer. You would not want to call the manufacturer to order potato chips, canned goods, vegetables, screwdrivers, etc. In this case, the customer would contact the warehouse and order a series of products for direct delivery. Since preferences will be known through products like the smart card, some of these orders, such as food products, can be automatic.

The impact of this change on retail operations can be devastating. The companies that insist on retaining the costly middleman function will not be able to compete economically with the direct warehouse to consumer systems.

Companies that are currently in the retail business, no matter how profitable they are, will be viewed as being at risk. This will impact their valuation dramatically. Valuation these days is more a function of potential than of current performance. These retail businesses must seriously consider Internet selling using dynamic catalogues. Implementing this will be complex. Should the e-commerce business be spun off? Should it be set up initially as a separate entity? Hybrids (bricks and mortar plus e-commerce companies) are not yet given full recognition in terms of valuation. Should the company create its own e-commerce business or should it utilize the strong e-commerce capability of companies like Amazon.com? If this transition is done correctly, it could add millions of dollars to the value of the business. If it is done incorrectly, millions of dollars in valuation will be left needlessly on the table, only to be picked up by another company.

3. **The Collapse Of Administrative Layers** — The previous industrial revolution dramatically reduced the cost of manufacturing a product. However, because the mass-produced product was standardized, significant dollars had to be spent in marketing and advertising to convince the customer to buy the product. The new technology will allow the consumer to customize and get exactly what he/she wants, then have the product delivered efficiently.

   This new industrial revolution will finish the task of reducing costs by collapsing the layers of marketing, distribution and administration. Organizations of the future will be flatter as we eliminate and automate all repetitive work including repetitive logical thinking. The management of the future will spend more of their

workday in the creative area and less time pushing information and pieces of paper from one side of the desk to
the other.

4. **Consumers Online** — Consumers are moving online
at an even more rapid pace as they begin to use personal computers. As the Baby Boomer generation takes
hold, there will be greater computer literacy, less fear of
the computer and recognition of the significant benefits
of using the Internet. The variety of services being
offered will be enormous. More buying by consumers
on the Internet will signal a fundamental change in
retailing practices across the developed world. The
Internet will, in effect, become a huge online catalogue.
As the bandwidth capacity increases, it will include video
and 3D graphics and will allow the consumer to interact
with the website to have important questions answered
online. The postage and printing costs of direct marketing will be virtually eliminated. Since this represents
their greatest expense, such companies will have
increased profits and will pass on some of these economic benefits to the consumer. Many time consuming
tasks will be greatly reduced. Instead of driving around
the neighborhood looking for real estate with a broker,
consumers can find out directly which houses are currently for sale. Then they can take a virtual tour of the
house before deciding if a visit is necessary. We will be
able to contact professionals such as consultants,
attorneys, accountants and the like online via the
Internet.

Who will benefit from all of this? Companies like
UPS and Federal Express come to mind. Who will lose?
— brokers and many exclusively "bricks and mortar"
retail operations.

As consumers move online, they will want more
sophisticated and powerful computers, thereby

increasing demand in that category.

5. **Automation Of Left Brain Corporate Activities** —
Possibly the most significant impact of technology will
be the change in the role of management. Top management must identify clearly the tasks they perform that
are programmable. This will eliminate the shuffling of
paper and the enormous amount of wasted time spent
trying to track what is happening. Stock exchanges, for
example, can run themselves using very sophisticated
decision rules that can be predetermined by the key
executives. This frees up executives to be creative, establish business strategies, set goals and objectives, organize
activities, evaluate merger and acquisition opportunities
and evaluate personnel.

The network organization can deliver products and
services on a day-to-day basis with minimal interaction
on the part of management. The change is dramatic. It
will mean the end of much of today's middle management. It also will mean the end of many selling functions because the network organization can respond
directly to consumer needs. No longer will it be necessary to convince the consumer to buy the company's
standardized product. Top down management will also
come to an end. Employees will make decisions for
consumers directly. Specialists who have complete
knowledge about a given product, in turn, will back up
these employees. We are already seeing this happen in
the catalogue companies. Ideas such as reengineering
miss the point. Reengineering still works fundamentally
with a top down management concept. Management
will not change to this network organization easily.
Those companies who do not see the light soon will be
bypassed by those who do.

This requires a complete change in the corporate
culture. The change is bound to meet a high level of

resistance until management acknowledges that it has no choice if it is to compete effectively.

WHERE DO WE GO FROM HERE?

Corporations must engage experts in the field of **Value Creation**, not only to maximize value, but also to survive. Knowledge of the company's *core* business will not be enough. The **Value Creation** specialist must: understand how the technology revolution impacts your business; know where *all* the available sources of capital and debt are located; know where the talent is located to implement a paradigm shift; and understand the economic environment and the impact all changes will have on the company's operations, marketing, organization and strategic planning. Executives will have to move out of their area of comfort into a world where they have little expertise. They need to work as a team with **Value Creation** experts to move to the next level. There is little time to waste. During this decade, the Baby Boomers will reach their peak spending period. Consumers will be computer literate and will be moving online in record numbers. Comfortable with the new technology, they will avoid companies that are not at the cutting edge. The new consumer will want speed and quality at the best price. Customer loyalty may become a thing of the past for certain types of products. Companies that are waiting for a return of the *good old days* are in for a great disappointment.

The changes described will affect the mid-market companies ($10 million to $1.5 billion) profoundly. Ignoring or minimizing the impact of these changes is a sure formula for disaster. On the other hand, recognizing these changes and incorporating them into your business is not only the proper defensive action, but could create significant opportunity for **Value Creation**.

Each executive must first examine his/her *core* business.

Then comes the more difficult task of creating a paradigm shift, often to businesses and products outside of the executive's *comfort zone*. At the current rate of change and obsolescence, time and procrastination are the enemies to overcome. This is particularly true if the business is currently doing well, even though dark clouds are appearing on the horizon.

Chapter 5

The Preliminary Assessment

Before any company embarks on a program of **Value Creation**, it is important to determine whether or not there is an opportunity to increase the worth of the business dramatically. Restructuring the *core* business so that a breakthrough can be achieved will create value. This task involves looking for opportunities to increase the revenue generating capacity or to implement cost reductions that exceed the 20 percent per annum range. This is not easy, and the improved profitability that will be realized most likely will be subject to the existing multiple of EBIT (earnings before interest and taxes) or earnings per share that the company has experienced in the past.

A company can also create value by considering paradigm shifts that, in fact, increase the multiple of the business, giving it a greater perceived future value. General Electric and General Motors are good cases in point. The price/earnings multiple for General Electric varies, but is often over forty (40) times earnings. The price/earnings multiple for General Motors more often than not is under ten (10). This is because the market believes that General Electric will experience a higher rate of growth and profitability in the future than General Motors. One way or another, the market evaluates what a business will look like over the next three to five years, brings this back to the present value and assigns some sort of discount for uncertainty. This process is an art form. The market is subject to all sorts of other impacts, such as the perceived condition of the economy, future legislation, international conflicts, politics, interest rates, availability of capital, new taxes, etc. However, I believe that over time, the market will reflect the intrinsic value of the business.

In a preliminary evaluation, the first task is to review the *core* business. The process also will reveal the limitations of the company. Such an assessment would include reviews of:

- Financials and operating reports;

- Personnel and facilities;

- Products and services;

- Efficiency and effectiveness of operations and procedures;

- Marketing and sales strategy;

- Cash flow, cash needs and balance sheet strength;

- Existing strategic planning;

- Strengths and weaknesses of the business;

- Sources of capital for growth; and

- Management limitations.

The overview will help to identify areas of probable savings in the *core* business. Quantifying a range of savings along with the necessary investment in resources will assist in determining whether a given *core* project makes economic sense. From this first part of the assessment, management will gain an idea of expected benefits.

The second part of the analysis focuses on paradigm shifts to increase the earnings multiple. This is basically a creative effort in which it is important to think "out of the box." The ideas generated would be converted into projects. Each project would be evaluated on a preliminary basis utilizing the following information:

- Expected savings;

- Investment in human resources;

- Direct monetary investment;

- Time frame;

- Responsibilities; and

- Probability of success.

The projects could include but not be limited to:

- Utilizing technology to either reduce costs or generate revenue, e.g. Internet marketing;

- Selecting acquisitions that could dramatically change the perception of the company;

- Selling off portions of the business that are a "drag" on its value;

- Building the infrastructure needed to support massive expansion;

- Entering the global marketplace;

- Developing key strategic alliance partners; and

- Building the organization and leadership team that can direct future growth.

After this effort has been completed and each project has been analyzed on a preliminary basis, management can determine whether there appears to be a basis for more detailed study. In most cases, there are innumerable opportunities that must be looked at in great detail.

6

Development Of The Value Creation Plan

Up to this point, we have clarified our goals and objectives, determined where we are on the **Corporate Clock**, become acquainted with the available technology that is out there and looked at ways in which we might make use of it in the near future. It is time to develop the Plan itself. This is both a right and left brain process. Some areas, such as evaluating purchasing, distribution, and the need for certain products and/or services, can be subjected easily to organized rational thinking in order to arrive at a decision. Other areas, such as timing for globalization, joint ventures, strategic alliances, and the like, involve a good deal of creativity in addition to knowledge beyond the *core* business of the company. The proper talent must be assembled to begin this process properly. The minimal team should include:

- An accountant who can evaluate the economic impact of the various projects to make certain they are financially feasible;

- A high tech expert who understands the problems, costs

and general feasibility of making use of the many technologies that exist;

- A marketing or sales executive who understands the competitive environment in the *core* business;

- An outsider or qualified outside Board member who understands the overall business and economic environment;

- An MIS executive to determine how these various projects, once implemented, can be controlled;

- An operational type who understands how all elements of the cost and infrastructure side of the business operate; and

- An investment banker or Wall Street type if capital is to be raised or there is consideration of going public.

Another precondition for developing a Value Creation Plan is the establishment of the proper environment. What does that environment look like?

1. The CEO supports the process 100%.

2. Middle management is convinced that change is needed. This is not merely a curious exercise.

3. Management is clear about its own goals and objectives.

4. The proper talent has been assembled as outlined above.

5. The talent has the time to perform the **Value Creation** project without sacrificing the efficient running of the

core business.

6. There is an understanding and consensus related to where the existing business is on the **Corporate Clock**.

7. The company is not in a **Crisis** or **Conflict** mode.

Unless the CEO has committed to being actively involved in the Plan and to push it along, it is a waste of time and effort. His/her involvement is extremely important in accomplishing Item #2 above. Knowing that the CEO wants the Plan to become a reality will help middle management's *hearts and minds* to participate. However, if the commitment of middle management is to be real, they must see the idea of a **Value Creation Plan** as congruent with their own personal goals and objectives. Otherwise, they may take passive aggressive steps to block the progress of the Plan. While it is essential to the support of management, the **Value Creation** committee must have the skills identified above. The blending of inside and outside knowledge produces the best results. The development of a **Value Creation Plan** takes time. Various projects will have to be studied to determine their feasibility. Many will be aborted in the early stages, others abandoned later. A few good ones will remain. All of this takes time. This **Value Creation** project process occurs at the same time that the *core* business is in operation and in need of management's attention. This organizational problem must be worked out, but can only be solved at the top.

Finally, there must be some consensus about the existing **health** of the business. If middle management thinks everything is okay just the way it is, it will be almost impossible to bring about change.

Item #7 in the above list is meant to emphasize that you can't install a **Value Creation** program when the company is in trouble. First, the problem must be fixed and the business brought to a **Healthy** state.

Now we are ready to develop the **Value Creation Plan**. Discussed below are some of the categories that probably will require investigating.

CLARIFICATION OF MANAGEMENT OBJECTIVES

A **Value Creation Plan** cannot be created in a vacuum. There are often conflicting goals that must be sorted out.

A client of ours heads one-third of a company that resulted from a merger of three mid-size companies: one located in the west, one in the east and one in the mid-west. As time passed, the owner of the western operation announced that he wanted to exit in three to five years. The owner of the eastern operation was indifferent, but the mid-west owner wanted to retain the business (or at least his original business) indefinitely. We worked out a way to let the mid-western operation be *spun-off,* leaving the rest of the business to be prepared for sale so that we could concentrate on value maximization.

Even when there is only one owner, the objectives must be clear. If, for example, the goal was to retain the business through the creation of a family dynasty or by hiring professional management, then value would not be determined based on the sale of the business, but rather on the maximization of cash flow and profits. The issue of improving the earnings multiple would be less significant.

If the owner wants to sell the business, value maximization would take a different course. The time frame, three to five years versus ten years, would affect the approach. In one case, the owner would have to consider acquisitions, joint ventures and strategic alliances. However, if there were sufficient time, he/she could develop some of the capabilities required to create value internally.

Whether to go public or execute a private sale should be considered in terms of timing, attitude about cash versus stock and concern about liability. There are times when you can keep control and meet liquidity goals by either raising capital or going public, *if those are* your objectives. Do you want to exit completely, or do you just want to reallocate the assets in your estate to provide for greater liquidity?

This is the first step in the development of the **Value Creation Plan**. The discussion in Chapter Two should be of great assistance.

DEVELOPMENT OF PRELIMINARY TARGETS

Once the goals are defined, dates and numbers must be analyzed. If the goal is to sell the business for $100 million, the business is currently worth $100 million, *and* everyone wants to exit as soon as possible, the solution is simple. Sell the company now by developing a first class package. Perhaps the *Book* on the company can add some value through proper positioning of the business, but there is little **Value Creation** to be done.

If, however, the current business is worth $60 million and the goal is $100 million, then $40 million of value has to be created. If this existing business has an EBITDA (earnings before interest, tax, depreciation, and amortization) multiple of 6, then $40 million of increased value requires an increase in EBITDA of about $6.7 million. If, however, the company, through **Value Creation** can command an EBITDA multiple of 10, the new EBITDA goal would be $10 million to achieve a value of $100 million. Since the company's EBITDA was $10 million at a multiple of 6, it does not have to increase earnings. Instead, it must change the buyer's perception of value by entering businesses with high growth rates and profit potential.

Once the dollar targets are established, the next key question is timing. The more time that is available before exiting, the easier the transition to the new value.

The second step answers the questions of *how much* and *when* for those who want to exit.

If the business is being retained, then cash flow and profit targets should be established, along with a staged timing program for management transition.

Exhibit B illustrates a company that needs to create $45 million in increased value to meet their target of $125 million. The business had an EBITDA multiple of 7 which would have required $6.4 million of incremental EBITDA to meet the target. If we succeed in increasing the EBITDA multiple to 15, we would require only $3.0 million in incremental EBITDA to meet the goal. In other words, by making the correct paradigm shifts, the company could meet its goal with $3.4 million less in incremental earnings.

ADDITION AND DELETION OF PRODUCTS AND SOURCES

An important early step in the **Value Creation** process is to evaluate all products and services to determine if they should be deleted because:

• They do not produce sufficient (or any) profit; and

• They have a negative impact on the earnings multiple.

In cases where the product or service has a positive impact on the earnings multiple but is not profitable, it is necessary to determine whether operational changes can be made. If there is no reasonable way to improve profit performance for a product or service, even if it could have a positive impact on the earnings multiple, it is best to delete and move on to greener pastures. At the same time, the business may be capable of adding products or services that would drive the revenue and improve the multiple.

EXHIBIT B
IMPACT OF EBITDA MULTIPLE ON COMPANY VALUE

INCREMENTAL EBITDA	CHANGE IN COMPANY VALUE						
	5x MULTIPLE	7x MULTIPLE	8x MULTIPLE	10x MULTIPLE	15x MULTIPLE	20x MULTIPLE	25x MULTIPLE
$500,000	$2,500,000	$3,500,000	$4,000,000	$5,000,000	$7,500,000	$10,000,000	$12,500,000
$1,000,000	$5,000,000	$7,000,000	$8,000,000	$10,000,000	$15,000,000	$20,000,000	$25,000,000
$1,500,000	$7,500,000	$10,500,000	$12,000,000	$15,000,000	$22,500,000	$30,000,000	$37,500,000
$2,000,000	$10,000,000	$14,000,000	$16,000,000	$20,000,000	$30,000,000	$40,000,000	$50,000,000
$2,500,000	$12,500,000	$17,500,000	$20,000,000	$25,000,000	$37,500,000	$50,000,000	$62,500,000
$3,000,000	$15,000,000	$21,000,000	$24,000,000	$30,000,000	$45,000,000	$60,000,000	$75,000,000
$3,500,000	$17,500,000	$24,500,000	$28,000,000	$35,000,000	$52,500,000	$70,000,000	$87,500,000
$4,000,000	$20,000,000	$28,000,000	$32,000,000	$40,000,000	$60,000,000	$80,000,000	$100,000,000
$4,500,000	$22,500,000	$31,500,000	$36,000,000	$45,000,000	$67,500,000	$90,000,000	$112,500,000
$5,000,000	$25,000,000	$35,000,000	$40,000,000	$50,000,000	$75,000,000	$100,000,000	$125,000,000

HYPOTHETICAL EXAMPLE:

Company's Current Value	$ 80 mil
Company's Target Value	$125 mil
Desired Value Increase	$ 45 mil

EBITDA Multiple:	5x	7x	8x	10x	15x	20x	25x
Required change in EBITDA to achieve desired $45 mil value increase:	$9.0 mil	$6.4 mil	$5.6 mil	$4.5 mil	$3.0 mil	$2.3 mil	$1.8mil

I must be clear that, at this juncture, we are talking only about additions that utilize existing facilities and are well within the financial and human resource capability of the organization. Our objective at this juncture is to maximize value without making massive changes to the business.

SELLING OFF PORTIONS OF THE BUSINESS

There may be segments of the business that are losing money and cannot be brought to profitability in the near future. It may be best to package and sell them. There also may be portions of the business that are profitable and do well, but command low earning multiples because: perceived growth potential is limited; there is excessive competition; or the product has moved from proprietary to a commodity. Most important, this segment of the business is dragging down the multiple of the entire business. Sometimes it is best to package and sell this portion.

This step generally requires a longer lead-time than adding and deleting products because management usually has less experience in this area. Selling a business involves creating a *Book* which usually includes:

- Forecasted financials;

- Supporting assumptions;

- Management and organization;

- Risks;

- Existing competition;

- Marketing strategy; and

• Existing financial with supporting narrative.

The *Book* would be delivered to potential buyers. Will they be strategic or financial buyers? If the buyer is a competitor, will access to information present a problem? Meetings, determination of value, and the complex task of financial structuring follow this. Will it be a stock deal? All cash? Is there an earn-out component, etc.? It is best to get started as early as possible.

MAKING SELECTIVE ACQUISITIONS

If there is enough lead-time and sufficient financial capability, selective acquisitions can make a difference, particularly by increasing the earnings multiple.

A client of ours owned a large *bricks and mortar* retail chain which, while profitable, commanded an earnings per share multiple of about 8 times. We identified a large company doing catalogue and Internet selling that was about 1/3 the size of the retail chain that was losing money. We could see how easy it would be to bring it to profitability through the merger. We were able to make a stock deal on favorable terms. Within six months, we brought this new Internet and on-line catalogue business to profitability, creating an increase in value resulting from increased earnings. More importantly, the combined entity now commanded a multiple of 14 times earnings, which had the greatest impact on valuation.

The objective of making selective acquisitions is to look for businesses that increase overall earnings of the merged entity or increase the earnings multiple of the merged entity because the new business has a higher anticipated growth rate.

We also need to identify businesses where there is a high motivation to sell. When the motivation is high, the price is favorable, and the chances of success are higher. These could include the following:

- Aging ownership;

- Financial problems;

- Illness or disability of owner;

- High management turnover; and

- Conflicts between major shareholders.

The acquisition option, of course, has to be compared with in-house development of a given capability. The answer is related to timing and the risk versus reward tradeoff.

There is also a skill in maximizing the value of the entity to be sold.

We recently represented a company that was selling its tool division. They hoped to get $8.0 million for the business. By the time the process was completed, they received $14 million for a business that had a history of non-profitability. What did we do?

Specific Value Enhancements:

1. We prepared a comprehensive sales memo describing the company.

2. We identified profitability enhancements such as:

   - Relocation of the aerospace from the construction division; and

   - Growth possibilities for the plant facilities.

3. We identified specific buyers in industries that provided a strategic fit. These included the automotive industry and other industrial companies.

4. We expanded the brand name into other tools such as electric, hydraulic and gas-powered.

5. We cultivated competitive bids among several buyers in selected industries.

6. We needed to show that future profits were expected along with reasonable growth.

7. We also needed to create competition between the buyers.

ANALYZING FINANCIAL RESTRUCTURING

Often, in the early stages of building a business, when money is short, management will go to any length to generate capital. The stockholders' equity section is burdened with many options, warrants, redeemable preferred, convertible preferred, different classes of common, convertible debt and the like. The complexity alone is enough to scare off would-be buyers. If the buyer is willing to wade through a complex equity structure, it will be at a price. They will assume all options. Warrants will be exercised in the future so that "fully diluted" earnings per share may be quite a bit lower than earnings per share of common stock outstanding. The buyer also will give the most detrimental interpretation of convertible stock and debt.

Therefore, it is always wise to simplify the capital and debt structure of the company in advance. This process, often poorly understood, involves negotiation with equity and debt holders. The ability to simplify depends on (1) availability of cash; and (2) the recognition on the part of equity holders that the simplification process is in their best interest. There are accounting and legal ramifications in the process of simplification beyond the scope of this book. Suffice it to say that financial restructuring needs to be given careful consideration.

BUILDING INFRASTRUCTURE TO SUPPORT MASSIVE EXPANSION

This can best be explained by example. I will call this real client by the fictional name of ABC Distribution, Inc.

ABC Distribution, Inc. distributes computers, printers, fax machines and consumables to the retail electronics industry.

ABC Distribution's annual 100% growth rate had stripped the owner of his ability to control operations. When we arrived, unfilled orders averaged 100 per day. Working capital was insufficient. Operation systems such as inventory control, order entry, warehouse management and financial controls were either nonexistent or functioned inadequately. Warehouse and office facilities were inadequate for an operation of this size.

There was a siege mentality among senior managers. Fighting fires, along with constant **crisis** management and damage control, was the norm rather than the exception. Such a style is typical of companies with a project orientation rather than one that is process oriented. In this case, the company's infrastructure couldn't keep up with the current pace of the business.

If correctly filled orders didn't start shipping on time, the company was in danger of losing its largest customers. Worse still, ABC Distribution's largest vendor was concerned about the company's performance and fiscal stability.

By this time, the two owners wanted to cash out. They engaged an investment banker to sell the company. The banker felt that a realistic price for the company was less than half of what the two owners thought appropriate. No offers were tendered by the banker's contacts. We immediately stabilized the company to stop customers and vendors from leaving and created a paradigm shift to add value to prospective buyers.

Our first task, stabilizing the company, allowed us just four weeks to turn around an operation that was out of control. We focused on shipping and warehouse operations. The objective was to eliminate the backlog of unfilled orders. The problems were solved in less than a month.

Concurrently, we fixed the order monitoring mechanism that allowed management to identify backlogs and deal with them before they became crises. Presentations and an on-site review for the major customers and the vendor, as well as the company's newly improved performance, allowed ABC Distribution to save these relationships. Without them, they probably would not have survived.

The second challenge required the owners and employees to change their approach to managing the business. This set the stage for the value-added work needed to double the company's sale price. These significant paradigm shifts led them to:

- **Employ A Management Team** — Prior to our involvement, management was homegrown and employed a *seat of the pants* style of running the company. The extensive and sophisticated changes required installing a professional management team that was up to the task of doubling size and increasing profitability.

- **Install Management Systems** — Adding value for potential buyers required installing an infrastructure of systems and controls that allowed the company to grow operationally.

- **Cement Customer Relationships** — The company needed to secure its place in both their vendor and customer relationships — in an industry that characteristically avoids formal attachments.

- **Increase Profit Margins** — Virtually doubling the company's value meant that we had to raise EBITDA and net profits to a level where buyers could get a return worth their risk for a price the owners felt should be "something north of $100 million." The revolutionary new DEF division helped raise profits by changing the company's traditional relationship with vendors from that of distributor to a true business partner and brand manager.

- **Grow Revenue** — Distribution companies make money on their thin profit margins by significantly increasing sales. For the company, this meant at least doubling the company's revenue. Before we began, revenue was $438 million. This meant that we would have to increase revenue to over $1 billion annually.

- **Improve Earnings Quality** — The company was overly dependent on just one vendor and three customers for over 75% of their sales. This undue concentration reduced the perception of earnings quality. It had to be fixed.

- **Begin Long Range Planning** — To position the company where the owners wanted it, they had to establish a formal program of long range planning. This included specific assignments to individuals given the authority to make decisions, the responsibility to make the right decisions, and accountability for the results.

What were these infrastructure improvements? Over an eight-month period, we established a value-added program designed to raise the company's sale price. Revenue exceeded $1.5 billion last year and will exceed $2.0 billion next year. The owners have a business valued over $200 million. This is four times the value at the start of the **Value Creation** project.

Many companies have the ability to grow to a size much larger than the level contemplated by management. This requires a paradigm shift in thinking, a new vision and the talent to build the infrastructure necessary to handle the growth without being overwhelmed.

DETERMINING FEASIBILITY AND TIMING FOR GLOBALIZATION

As pointed out in Chapter Four, the new technology will enable mid-size companies to participate in the global marketplace. At one time, these international markets were only available to the major corporations. We believe I^2 will significantly reduce the cost of entry for these mid-market companies.

As the developing nations come on board, they will have to make major investments in infrastructure. This means roads, highways, airports, bridges, manufacturing facilities and the like. The information highway will make it easier to connect with Western Europe, Taiwan, South Korea and Singapore. As the developing nations continue to expand, there will be a growth of the middle class, which will demand more goods and services. The mid-market companies need to evaluate the needs of the international market and match them with their *core* competencies.

Adding an international component to a business can dramatically increase its potential market so that its perceived growth rate will be enhanced. This, in turn, not only increases revenue and profits, but also will have a positive impact on the earnings multiple and the value of the business.

EVALUATING JOINT VENTURES, OUTSOURCING AND STRATEGIC ALLIANCES

It is not always possible to acquire another company, nor is it always the best way to leverage a company. Joint ventures and strategic alliances work well when there is a high degree of trust between the parties, and there is a clear-cut mutual benefit. They quickly fall apart when they are one-sided. No matter how carefully the agreements are drafted, if one side perceives that they are unfair, they will find a way to terminate the relationship. It is important to be certain that your joint venture or strategic alliance partner does not have businesses that compete directly with you, or you may just be *educating* a new competitor. If your partner is too powerful, this could lead to a takeover in which you may have shared valuable information that may impede your ability to negotiate.

Good partnerships work because each side realizes an increased level of business through the venture or alliance and discovers that they can trust each other.

Look for long-term potential and backup plans. It would be counterproductive to **Value Creation** to have ventures and alliances with short life spans.

Outsourcing can provide great flexibility by transforming functions to more efficient partners. Outsourcing also provides flexibility in adjusting to downturns in the business and eliminates the headache of addressing personnel and other operating issues. Just be careful that you have not become dependent on the outsource partner. In fact, no matter how good that partner is, it is better to have more than one source; otherwise, you are not only vulnerable, but you ultimately lose your leverage in negotiating price.

ASSURING OPTIMAL USE OF THE INFORMATION HIGHWAY

I suggest a more careful reading of Chapter Four. The information highway has many ruts and sharp protruding objects. It can be costly to incorporate it in your business and may not produce results. However, ignoring its impact can result in your ultimate demise. It can generate new revenue, but sometimes at too great a cost. It can also save money, if you know what you're doing.

RAISING OF CAPITAL OR DEBT

Sometimes, in order to take the business to the next level in terms of value, it is necessary to raise capital. This is a complex issue that depends on the need for control, the condition of the marketplace and the timing requirements. In this brief section, let me identify a few possibilities.

- **Asset-based Lenders** — These lenders will often make loans on less desirable deals if the loan can be secured by the assets of the business and the assets of the owners.

- **Banks** — Traditionally, banks will provide lines of credit based on cash flow that usually require the businesses to be in an "out of debt" position once every 12 months. They will also make loans and often look for personal guarantees when dealing with the mid-market. See my book, *How To Turn Around A Financially Troubled Company* (McGraw Hill, 1982), on the issue of guarantees.

- **Going Public** — If this is feasible and the market conditions are right, it solves the problem of acquiring capital for the business and liquidity for the shareholders at the same time. It will cost many hundreds of thousands of dollars (sometimes over a million) in legal and accounting fees and can take from six months to one year to implement.

- **Private Placement Through Institutional Sources** — Funds from this source can be obtained more quickly when market conditions are right. These institutions are run by sophisticated people who generally value your business at less than the public market.

- **Private Placement Through Private Sources** — When the funds needed are not significant ($1 to $5 million), funds can be raised from wealthy individuals. Often, they are less demanding, so disclosure documents must be complete. If for any reason the business fails to perform, they are more likely to take legal action. However, they will generally give the company a higher valuation than the institutional sources.

- **Venture Funds** — These funds already possess the capital. It is the responsibility of the fund managers to deliver a high rate of return for their investors. They are very sophisticated and will perform careful due diligence before making an investment. In general, they are conservative in valuing the business, but they can move rapidly once they decide they like your company.

LOCATING THE MANAGEMENT EXPERIENCE NEEDED TO SUPPORT THE NEW PRODUCTS AND SOURCES

It is a mistake to think that a business can venture into new areas using the existing management. These companies believe that they need to hire only lower level personnel, who will be supervised by the current executives. When a company ventures into a new area, such as Internet selling for example, they need to hire a top executive who has a proven track record in Internet selling. Only he/she will know how to hire and control competent subordinates. If you are going to pursue international markets, you need an executive who knows how to sell to different cultures with different values and, in some cases, a different code of ethics as it relates to business.

Failure to bring in the new top management (with a track record) will negatively impact value in the following ways:

- Investors, buyers and underwriters will not believe you can make a success of the new business in a reasonable time frame — or at all!

- Apart from the perception issue discussed above, the business is unlikely to make it because the top management experience necessary for success will not exist. Ego is the big enemy. Often top management cannot accept its limitations.

DEVELOPING A PUBLIC DISCLOSURE PLAN

The company has determined the **Value Creation** strategy and has made sufficient implementation progress so that it is confident about the success, timing and milestones of the Plan. It is now time to communicate the Plan to all members of the outside and inside communities who have a need to know. Listed below are some of the important elements that must be communicated:

- You have recreated your business to maximize value.

- All elements of your business have enormous growth potential.

- You will be dominant in the markets you selected.

- The management talent is in place to carry out the Plan.

- You have the financial resources to carry out the Plan.

- You have a vision of the future and can clearly articulate that vision.

- You have the infrastructure to manage what you are creating.

When this effort is completed, millions of dollars will have been added to the value of your business, and the primary responsibility of maximizing the value of the business to shareholders will have been achieved.

INSTALLING INCENTIVE PROGRAMS

If top management is committed to **Value Creation**, its measurement must be based on the incremental value created. Some top executives of public companies understood this concept and asked to be rewarded, not on the basis of profit improvement, but on the basis of increased value. They saw, as their main objective, the increase in shareholder value and tied their bonus to a very small percentage of the increase in value created under their regime. Other executives were rewarded on a similar basis. This is a far cry from fixed bonuses, bonuses based on meeting or exceeding budget, and the like.

If we want an organization and management team devoted to maximizing value, we need to reward on that basis. Many executives believe that their major task is to maximize profits and that value is in the *hands of the gods*. Executives who believe this and desire rewards on this basis will always be a detriment to implementing a successful **Value Creation Plan**.

CHANGING THE ORGANIZATION STRUCTURE

Organizing incorrectly can have disastrous effects, even on major corporations. Success can lead to a feeling of omnipotence, a feeling that all you have to do is produce the product or deliver the service and the customers will be there.

IBM's failure in the 1980's and early 1990's is a lesson in point. To the company's credit, it made a successful comeback, but what happened? The company lost its roots along the way, built a large hierarchical structure that slowed down decision-making and made communication from bottom to top extremely difficult. IBM was a one-stop shop, renting equipment to customers, supporting them and keeping these customers on the cutting edge. Employee loyalty was paramount. Yet, it misjudged the importance of the mainframe computer and missed the impact of the microcomputer. It could have purchased Microsoft easily in the early years, but did not see it as a threat. The company expected to grow to an enormous size on their old paradigm and built the organizational infrastructure to carry out this vision of growth. Some believe they began to see sales and marketing as a necessary evil and thought they could dictate to customers. In the 1960's IBM was a marketing company. Then they shifted from rentals to leases which were booked as sales. By 1985, they began to realize their strong performance was largely a bubble from the sell off of rental equipment. The top executive tried to manage from the top down, ignoring the important relationship with customers that had been built up over the years. Decision making was slow and based on consensus. There were too many meetings focusing on ideas and plans and not on operating results. Their full employment practice became a refuge for poor performers. This could not work in an environment of rapidly changing technology. Inbred executives were steeped in the arrogance of success.

I believe there are important lessons to learn from the IBM story about organization. In the process of implementing a **Value Creation Plan**:

- Remember your corporate strengths and your relationship with your *core* customers. It is these customers that produce the revenue.

- Do not violate your contract with your employees, but always be performance based.

- The competition is always changing. Part of your organization must pay serious attention to where your industry is going.

- Never build a top down organization structure. It is inefficient and does not empower middle management. Decisions should be made by those closest to the action.

- Remember that the Edsel was built by *consensus*.

- Don't inbreed. When you enter new business areas, find new leaders from the outside. Have a reasonable balance between insiders and outsiders.

- Remember, you cannot dictate to customers in the long run. Therefore, remain strong in marketing, sales and service.

- Look to absorb smaller companies that may be a threat in the future.

- Avoid excessive meetings. Have few scheduled meetings. Meet when there is something to talk about and emphasize performance.

- Avoid too many layers of management and too many executives. Limit the levels of management to a maximum of five.

- Don't build your management and staffing in advance of actual performance. It is very expensive to inventory talent. Have a Plan for organizational expansion, but don't implement that Plan until the employees are needed.

- Ignore the old *span of control* theory that limited the amount of direct reports. The information highway has expanded management's capacity to supervise. This will avoid the building of mini-empires inside the organization.

RISK VERSUS REWARD ANALYSIS

In the final analysis, the **Value Creation Pan** will be comprised of specific recommendations:

- In the *core* business; and

- In the making of major paradigm shifts.

Each one of these recommendations can be converted into projects. Each project will have a time line, investment costs and an estimate of probable results. Management may not have the financial or human resources to make all the changes. They also may not have the will. As the recommendations move outside of management's comfort zone, there is a reluctance to proceed with the projects.

When all the ideas for the creation of value are assembled,

it is necessary to evaluate the risks involved and the potential rewards. Some changes need to be made rapidly to insure survival. Others can wait. Some are risky, yielding great potential rewards. While it is important to make changes, one should not "throw the baby out with the bath water." Here is a largely summarized version of what happened in a **Value Creation** study we undertook.

We provided consulting services to assess the current operation and determine management's options for **Value Creation** and Exit Strategy. The result was a strategy that increased value by $20 million. This assignment included three specific tasks:

Task 1

Rationalize Financial Numbers — We developed the management reports needed in key operating areas of the company. The focus of these financially oriented presentations was on revenue and costs to determine the profitability of specific operations for management decision-making.

The second part of this task was to organize the chart of accounts and information gathering mechanisms so that staff could create this information each month in a timely, accurate fashion.

Task 2

Set Decision Point — Consolidate the wholesale operation. We were to develop a Plan showing the financial and operational impact of consolidating the wholesale operations currently in Los Angeles and Orange Counties. The second phase of this task was to demonstrate where the consolidation should be located and the steps that needed to be taken to relocate the operation.

Task 3

Develop Automated Routing — We created a cost-effective system designed to optimize and manage routing. Once the system was identified, we implemented the software to realize the full benefit of the routing system.

Specific value enhancements and dollar amount of value added. We:

- Calculated the profitability of specific operations and lack of profitability in others.

- Identified essential financial indicators in each operation such as gross sales volume, cost of sales, processing, delivery costs and net income. Management never before had received this kind of information in a timely, accurate format.

- Distinguished results of the retail operation from those of the wholesale operation. Again, management had never seen this type of information before.

- Determined that profit margins were falling as incremental revenue rose.

- Made decision to consolidate processing operations from both Los Angeles and Orange Counties to Orange County only. Identified the personnel, plant and renovation issues associated with that decision. Savings from this decision were approximately $600,000 annually.

- Engineered decision regarding the consolidation of processing and delivery systems. The decision was to implement a cross-docking operation and consolidate processing while leaving delivery decentralized. This resulted in a 10% – 15% cost reduction in processing and delivery expenses.

- Created a paradigm shift in the sales staff customer orientation and commission structure. This resulted in expanded product penetration and improved profit margins.

- Succeeded in doubling the shelf life of their perishable product by controlling the atmosphere, instituting pre-paks and injecting inert gas into the packs. This allowed the company to expand their service area, thereby growing sales.

- Automated order processing which resulted in improved inventory control and dispatching.

- Reorganized management structure of this family owned and operated enterprise.

- Initiated a professional merit review system new to the previously benevolent family employment structure.

- Identified the Exit Strategy required to realize the added value of the company within the five-year time horizon.

- Showed the business, in particular the auction systems, how to utilize the Internet to save money.

- Identified acquisition candidates that would positively impact the earnings multiple.

CONCLUSION

As you can see, the **Value Creation** process can be quite extensive. It involves taking a step back, seeing the business as it really is, understanding the larger economic forces that are at work and knowing what to do about what you see. Failure to undergo this process could lead to business failure at one end of the spectrum and the leaving of millions of dollars of value at the other end.

The final choice, as always, is in the hands of top management.

Chapter 7

Implementation Of The Value Creation Plan

To be successful, implementation requires consideration of the following:

- The "buy in" of middle management;

- An understanding of the relationship between a project and process structure; and

- A monitoring, measuring and reporting system that keeps the program on track based on approved timetables.

We are assuming for purposes of this chapter that the "buy in" at the top executive level has been achieved. The program will cause disruption and some frustrating moments. The CEO must lead the charge and should be part of the **Value Creation Plan** implementation.

Let us look at some of these considerations in greater detail.

THE "BUY IN" OF MIDDLE MANAGEMENT

A plan is only a plan. This is true even for a **Value Creation Plan**. It must be implemented. As pointed out in Chapter Six, however, implementation will not occur if top and middle management do not buy into the Plan. If you have been diligent in following the recommended program, management at all levels will have been involved in the process from the start. Therefore, they will be part of the solution. The CEO must take the leadership. He/she must actually sell the Plan. This will not be an easy task because it will involve change.   Let's try to understand and be sympathetic to middle management by looking at a few examples:

1. **Adding And Deleting Of Products And Services** — This will impact the sales and marketing department whose orientation is related to the maximization of revenue, not to improving the earnings multiple. They will not understand why certain products or services, while profitable today, have limited future potential. Nor will they understand why getting into new products or services that may be initially unprofitable but have enormous potential makes any sense. It also will upset their current method of compensation.

2. **Selling Off Portions Of The Business** — This effort will strike fear in the hearts of all leaders of segments of the business as they see their compatriots sold off to another company. Management will have to make it clear which portions are going to be sold off and which are not. Employees need to understand and buy into the reasons for the sale.

3. **Making Selective Acquisitions** — The middle

managers initially will see these new businesses as competitors. The acquired company undoubtedly will have a different culture and may even be superior to the parent in certain areas. This area of superiority will worry middle management in the parent company. If, for example, the acquired company has an outstanding MIS department, the parent MIS department will feel threatened.

4. **Building Infrastructure To Support Expansion** — As the company upgrades inventory control, order entry, warehouse management and the like, certain employees may become obsolete. Similarly, when management deploys the information highway in other areas, e.g. finance and engineering, more people will be threatened. If action must be taken, it should be swift and decisive so that the remaining employees are assured of their jobs and positions.

5. **Determining Feasibility And Timing For Globalization** — Most employees are xenophobic. They think in terms of geographical regions and, in some cases, nationally. Their discomfort increases dramatically when the business moves onto foreign lands with foreign languages. We are a nation "from sea to shining sea." We border only two countries. One speaks our language. We are still uncomfortable with the other. There is a deep isolationist strain running through our culture. Top management has the task of helping employees feel comfortable with this change. The *global economy* and the need to be part of it are not easy to understand.

6. **Arranging Joint Venture, Outsourcing And Strategic Alliances** — The first middle management response to this aspect of the plan is, "Why can't we do

it ourselves?" Top management needs to explain that it is often uneconomical to try to be all things to all people. Joint ventures and alliances often can add to the value of a business but scare middle management. They will give the idea lip service, but inside they are worried. Their orientation is not to maximize the value of the business or to grow; it is rather to protect their turf. Management must let them know they are protected, if that is the case.

Outsourcing is particularly difficult. It can often mean the elimination of a whole department. "If it can happen to them, it can happen to me!" is the unexpressed thought. Middle management must be made to understand that there were unique reasons for deciding to outsource certain functions. These reasons do not apply to the other departments.

7. **Using The Information Highway To The Max —** This area, above all, frightens middle management because they do not understand the impact of technology on their business. However, the rate of change and therefore the rate of obsolescence is accelerating. The information highway is now impacting all aspects of business from sales, marketing and distribution to finance, administration and operations. In other words, no one is safe. When employees hear about fiber optics, bandwidth and I^2, smart cards, voice activation, video conferencing, customized software, embedded microprocessors and the like, they feel that soon they will be replaced by some machine or technology. It is important to familiarize your middle management with the effect technology will have on your business and on their jobs. They may need training to protect their positions, or they need to know that their jobs may be unaffected by technology. It is the task of top management to be sensitive, and to solve these problems.

8. **Locating The Management Experience Needed To Support The New Products And Services** — In the last chapter, we explained why it was important to locate new management with appropriate experience. The act of doing this, however, can cause great anxiety among existing management. Not only does this new management threaten their job security and perception of advancement but, in many cases, these new executives also command higher salaries in the marketplace. This issue cannot be ignored. If it is *swept under the carpet,* your business may lose its best people and retain the mediocre. In the final analysis, middle management wants to know how this change will affect them rather than why it is good for the company. Bringing in these new executives will also create a change in the corporate culture, which must be carefully managed.

9. **Installing Incentive Systems** — As pointed out in Chapter Six, middle management expects bonuses and other incentives for:

   • Showing up for work for another year;

   • Achieving certain revenue targets;

   • Achieving certain profit related targets; and

   • Controlling costs.

   When we reward based on managers' contributions to creating value, we upset the normal modus operandi for offering incentives.

   It is the responsibility of top management to define for each middle manager how the tasks they must complete relate to the creation of value. If, for example, locating a particular strategic alliance partner would enhance the value of the business, then the executive responsible for this task might be rewarded for locating the strategic partner and structuring the deal in an acceptable manner.

10. **Changing The Organization Structure** — It is generally always necessary to change the organization structure to maximize value. If there are too many executive posts or too many layers of management, certain positions will be eliminated, and there may not be a productive role for the people who filled those positions. We have found that it is best to make all the structural changes at once and attempt, if possible, to find roles for the dislocated executives. Once that process is completed, meet as soon as possible with the remaining executives to assure them that organizational structural changes have been completed.

As you can see from these ten examples, the psychological component of the implementation process cannot be ignored. Top management must address fear, anxiety and insecurity as early as possible. If this is not done, middle management will try to obstruct the **Value Creation** projects and attempt to make them fail or be aborted.

RELATIONSHIP BETWEEN A PROJECT AND PROCESS STRUCTURE

Assigning the implementation project to people who already have day-to-day responsibility in the organization is a guaranteed prescription for failure. You are adding this project onto their workload, and it will never get done. The **Value Creation** project must be established as a full-time organization with responsibility to see the process through to the end.

Here is a good way to look at the implementation:

| OLD COMPANY EXISTING OPERATIONS | VALUE CREATION PROJECT | NEW COMPANY |

As you can see from the above, the existing business (which I will call OLD COMPANY) continues in operation while the **Value Creation** team focuses on the implementation of the various projects in the Plan. The team will call upon OLD COMPANY executives selectively to assist in completing certain projects, paying careful attention not to overburden them. When all the projects have been completed, OLD COMPANY will be transformed seamlessly into NEW COMPANY. As described in Chapter Six, this team will transition into permanent positions (with the exception of outside professionals) once the implementation is complete. The team should report to the CEO directly so that he/she:

- Is current on the progress of the various projects;

- Can provide needed *horsepower* to push certain projects forward; and

- Can add to or reallocate resources as needed.

MONITORING, MEASURING AND REPORTING

Once the Plan is completed, each **Value Creation** project that is approved will:

- Have one individual responsible for that project reporting to the **Value Creation** team leader;

- Have an expense budget, by month, through the

completion of the project;

- Have important milestones to make certain progress is on track;

- Have an interim financial performance requirement prior to completion of the project; and

- Work with objective metrics to measure the success of the project.

The **Value Creation** leader will produce a weekly report that summarizes all of the projects, identifying which ones are on time, on budget and achieving the expected results.

I believe that companies that adopt **Value Creation** as part of their corporate culture will be the future successes, once the dust settles on the new economy. They will be the companies that made the necessary changes in a timely manner. The others will be left behind because they will not be able to compete effectively.

The ideas in this book have been tested and proven in the real world and I hope they spin you into action.

Chapter 8

The Exit Strategy Connection

While this is a book about **Value Creation**, it is impossible to ignore its connection to Exit Strategy. The two are inseparable. **Value Creation** should always precede exiting.

You have worked long and hard developing a valuable asset — your company. Earning each dollar was a struggle, but now it is time to think about how you exit from this business and convert it into a more liquid asset. Your friends in the locker room have many ideas for you to consider: "Sell it;" "Take it public;" "Bring in more capital;" "Bring in professional management and transition;" or, "Create a family dynasty." The ideas go on and on. Put yourself in the hands of a specialist, and he/she will sell you on his/her particular area of expertise. The real question is *"What do you want to accomplish?"* The answers are personal, psychological, and financial. Timing is very important. Timing is related both to the capital markets and to your personal needs. Frequently, the value of a business can be enhanced significantly before it is put on the market.

At the point where you begin to contemplate exit strategies, you need to look at all of these interactive considerations.

Like a complex jigsaw puzzle, the pieces must be put together so that you achieve your goals in the most economic manner with proper consideration for your personal goals. This analysis must be performed in a highly confidential manner so that a clear understanding of the wishes of the key parties is developed and preserved.

You have worked hard to accumulate net worth through your business. A poorly conceived or poorly executed decision can cost you millions of dollars. In the spirit of the successful achievement of economic and personal goals, I suggest that you remember the acronym **SMART** when contemplating an Exit Strategy program. Remember that the **M** in **SMART** is the **Value Creation Plan**.

There are five basic elements:

Setting up the basic foundation;

Maximizing the value of the business;

Assessing the options;

Rationalizing an Exit Strategy; and

Timing, timing and timing.

Setting Up The Basic Foundation — This has been carefully developed for you in Chapter Two.

Maximize The Value Of The Business — This involves the development of a **Value Creation Plan** as discussed in Chapter Five. When deciding to exit, it is important to maximize the value of the business before turning it over to a Mergers and Acquisitions Specialist.

Assessing The Options — Once the personal goals are understood, the potential for value maximization determined, and the legal and tax constraints evaluated, consideration of alternative exit strategies becomes the third crucial step. It is important at this juncture not to leap to a conclusion, but to study each of the options. We can often learn a great deal, even from those we reject. Consideration should be given to a variety of options, including the following:

- Going Public — through the front door;

- Going Public — through a reverse merger;

- Private Placement — through institutional sources;

- Private Placement — through private sources;

- Venture Capital and other Fund Investments;

- Strategic Partners;

- ESOP's and Management Buyouts;

- Merger;

- Sale of Business;

- Retaining Business — family dynasty;

- Retaining Business — professional management; and

- Other.

Detailed structuring of the deal is very important at this point. Some companies, lacking proper advice, have raised the needed capital but lost control of their business because of poor structuring.

Rationalizing **An Exit Strategy** — Based on the analysis in the assessment phase, select the option to be pursued. An operationally based Business Plan then must be developed. Its exciting narrative should emphasize management's understanding of the future potential of the business and its ability to move forward over the ensuing three to five years. The Plan should include the following:

- Integrated financial projections including a balance sheet, income statement, and statement of cash flow;

- Comprehensive assumptions to support the Plan;

- Staffing levels;

- Discussion of revenue and expense control;

- A summary of organization and personnel;

- Competitive summary; marketing strategy; risks of the business; and

- Summaries of other significant business issues.

The company would then develop the prioritized action steps to be taken to implement the Exit Strategy. The order is crucial. Premature distribution of information can be ineffective or even dangerous. Sources must be carefully contacted, and there is an *art* to the proper cultivation of these sources.

Timing, **Timing And Timing** — Before you move to implement this Exit Strategy, first consider the various factors which impact timing and the ultimate results:

- Personal goals may impact the timetable.

- The conditions of the capital markets may impact timing.

- The availability of personnel to do the "Dog and Pony Show" for the potential sources of funds could limit the speed of implementation.

- The availability of cash to fund the fees and expenses related to the program could be a major constraint.

- The financial condition of the company might dictate the timing.

- Certain future events in the marketplace, out of the control of management, may influence timing.

Developing and executing an Exit Strategy is a complex and subtle art. The Exit Strategy and its execution have a significant ongoing impact on an owner's post-transaction life. Whatever your strategy, it is first important to maximize the value of the business you plan to exit.

Index